YO-CYG-886

WITHDRAWN

No longer the property of the
Boston Public Library.
Sale of this material benefited the Library.

EMR

Purchased with State Funds

HEADQUARTERS:

BOSTON PUBLIC LIBRARY

The
American
Revolution

The American Revolution

Illustrated
with
photographs,
and maps
and drawings
by
Robert F. McCullough

DON LAWSON

America's
First War for
Independence

Abelard-Schuman
AN Intext PUBLISHER
New York
London

Library of Congress Cataloging in Publication Data

Lawson, Don.
  The American Revolution; America's first war for independence.

  (The Young people's history of America's wars)
  SUMMARY: Details the incidents provoking the American colonists' revolt against the British and the revolt itself which resulted in the forming of an independent nation.
  Bibliography: p.
    1. United States—History—Revolution, 1775–1783—Juvenile literature.
    [1. United States—History—Revolution, 1775–1783] I. McCullough,
  Robert F., 1929–   illus. II. Title.
  E208.L39   973.3   73–18545
  ISBN 0–200–00131–0

Copyright © 1974 by Don Lawson

All rights reserved. No part of this book may be reprinted, or reproduced or utilized in any form or by any electronic, mechanical or other means, now known or hereafter invented, including photocopying and recording, or in any information storage and retrieval system, without permission in writing from the Publisher.

New York	London
Abelard-Schuman	Abelard-Schuman
Limited	Limited
257 Park Avenue South	450 Edgware Road
10010	W2 1EG

Published on the same day in Canada by Longman Canada Limited.

Printed in the United States of America.

To Everett Sentman,
a friend indeed

—D.L.

BOOKS BY DON LAWSON

The Lion and the Rock
Young People in the White House, Revised Edition

THE YOUNG PEOPLE'S HISTORY OF AMERICA'S WARS series

The American Revolution
The Colonial Wars
The United States in the Korean War
The United States in World War I
The United States in World War II
The War of 1812

Contents

Illustrations

9

*Time Line
for the American
Revolution*

1764
April 5—Parliament passes Sugar Act (later repealed).

1765
March 22—Parliament passes Stamp Act (later repealed
but replaced by taxes on tea, glass etc.; these in turn
withdrawn in 1770, except for tax on tea).

1770
March 5—Boston Massacre.

1773
December 16—Boston Tea Party.

1775

March 23—Revolutionary convention at Richmond, Va; Patrick Henry's "Give me liberty, or give me death" speech.

April 19—Clashes between British redcoats and American Minutemen at Lexington and Concord.

May 10—Fort Ticonderoga taken by Colonels Ethan Allen and Benedict Arnold.

June 17—Battle of Breed's (Bunker) Hill.

July 3—Washington takes over command of Continental army.

November 12—Patriots take Montreal.

December 30–31—Patriots, under General Richard Montgomery and Colonel Benedict Arnold, defeated in attack on Quebec; Montgomery killed, Arnold wounded.

1776

March 16—Siege of Boston ends with British evacuation.

July 4—Declaration of Independence adopted.

August 27—Americans defeated by British on Long Island.

September 15—British occupy New York City.

September 22—Nathan Hale hanged.

October 28—Americans retreat from White Plains, New York.

November 16—British capture Forts Washington and Lee.

December 25–26—Washington launches surprise attack on Trenton, New Jersey.

1777

January 3—Washington wins victory at Princeton.

July 4–5—Fort Ticonderoga recaptured by British.

August 16—Hessians defeated near Bennington.

September 11—British win Battle of Brandywine.

September 26—British occupy Philadelphia.

October 4—Washington defeated at Germantown.

October 17—Burgoyne surrenders at Saratoga.

December 19—Washington's winter at Valley Forge begins.

1778

February 6—American-French alliance signed.

June 28—Battle of Monmouth.

December 29—George Rogers Clark recaptures Kaskaskia.

1779

February 23–25—Clark recaptures Vincennes.

June 21—Spain declares war on Great Britain.

July 6—"Mad Anthony" Wayne takes Stony Point.

September 23—John Paul Jones in the *Bonhomme Richard* captures the British warship *Serapis*.

1780

May 12—Charleston falls to British.

August 16—British win victory at Camden.

October 2—British Major John André hanged, following General Benedict Arnold's defection to the British.

October 7—American mountainmen take King's Mountain in south.

1781

January 17—Americans win at Cowpens in South Carolina.

March 15—Cornwallis and Greene battle indecisively at Guilford Courthouse, North Carolina.

September 5—French fleet drives away British fleet in Battle of the Chesapeake Capes.

October 19—Cornwallis surrenders at Yorktown.

1782

March 20—Lord North resigns.

July 11—British leave Savannah.

November 30—American-British preliminary peace treaty signed in Paris.

December 14—British leave Charleston.

1783

September 3—American-British final peace treaty signed in Paris.

November 25—British leave New York City.

"Young man, what we meant in going for those Red Coats was this: We always had governed ourselves, and we always meant to. They didn't mean we should."

—*Revolutionary War veteran*

One

The Boston
Massacre

For weeks there had been trouble brewing between the citizens of Boston and the so-called Boston Garrison, a detachment of British troops sent from England to maintain order in the rebellious city. On the cold, snowy evening of March 5, 1770, the trouble boiled over.

All day there had been minor incidents between bands of citizens and soldiers who roamed Boston's streets. That evening, a group of boys staged a mock snowball fight on King Street (today's State Street), where a lone British sentry was stationed near the Custom House.

Occasionally, a purposely misaimed snowball hit the sentry. Soon, some of the townspeople joined in the sport and commenced throwing snowballs, pieces of ice, sticks and stones at the red-coated target. When the group grew to nearly sixty tormentors, the sentry called for aid from the main garrison and about eight to ten British soldiers hurried to the scene.

Now the mob's anger grew, and clubs were added to the townspeople's weapons. The redcoats' threats to open fire were met by jeers and taunts for them to go ahead and do so. Some of the civilians even approached the soldiers and struck at their muskets with clubs. Suddenly shots rang out—it was never made clear if an order had been given to fire, or, if so, by whom—and three men lay dead and eight wounded, two of them mortally.

Those killed outright were identified by their Boston friends as James Caldwell, Samuel Gray, and Michael Johnson. Those mortally wounded were Patrick Carr and Samuel Maverick. Later it was learned that "Michael Johnson" was actually Crispus Attucks, a man thought by some to be partly or wholly Indian, a member of the nearby Natick tribe. Today, however, he is generally accepted as America's first black hero.

The events leading up to the "Boston Massacre"—as the tragic incident was quickly labeled by the Boston patriot and propagandist Sam Adams—had begun as far back as 1764, when the British Parliament passed the first of a series of acts designed to collect taxes from the American colonists. Great Britain had defeated the French in a long series of Colonial Wars for control of the North American continent,* and the British Parliament felt that the colonists should help pay for the cost of those wars. After all, the British reasoned, it was the colonists who would benefit most from the new era of

*See Volume I in this series.

The Spirit of '76 (Minor Congressional Committee in the National Archives)

peace and prosperity, so why shouldn't they help pay their own war debt?

In addition, hundreds of thousands of pounds sterling (a pound sterling was worth about $16.50) would have to be spent to man the forts vacated by the French at the close of the Colonial Wars. Additional money would be needed to maintain some twenty regiments of British troops to hold in check the Indians who were still under French influence and who might attack the colonists at any time. There were also a number of British administrators in the Thirteen Colonies whose salaries must be paid. Great Britain proposed to collect one-third of these costs from duties on American imports and from a stamp tax.

The colonists, on the other hand, disagreed with every tax levied on them by Great Britain's Parliament because, as they pointed out, they had no representatives in Parliament and thus had no voice in running their own private business affairs. "Taxation without representation is tyranny" was the way colonist James Otis bluntly put it. The British, however, believed that the colonists owed their allegiance to the Crown, or King George III, and so long as King George III said that Parliament's acts were legal and binding, the colonists had no say in the matter. There was very little doubt where King George III stood. He was squarely behind Parliament, stating that he would "rather risk his crown than stoop to opposition" from the American colonies. And if the people governed by Great Britain did not agree with him, "they shall have another king," he said. In the end it was this unreasonably stubborn attitude on the part of the king that backed the colonists into a corner, causing them to agree with one patriot's words, "Nothing will save us but acting together."

The Sugar Act, passed by Parliament on April 5, 1764, was the first parliamentary measure designed specifically to raise money from the colonies for Great Britain. The act was passed under the leadership of Prime Minister George Grenville, who had absolutely no understanding of the views of the colonists and flatly refused to concede that they had any political rights. Under this act, the colonists had to pay import duties on foreign molasses, sugar, wine, and certain similar goods. Also, to prevent smuggling, strong measures were adopted.

The Sugar Act, however, did not provide sufficient revenue, so Parliament passed further tax legislation, the Stamp Act, on March 22, 1765. This measure levied a direct tax on all colonial newspapers, many legal and commercial documents, pamphlets, ships' papers, insurance policies, and other kinds of circulating paper.

Parliament also passed a Quartering Act in March, 1765. This was the act that made each colony partly responsible for the expenses involved in maintaining British troops within that particular colony. The Quartering Act grew out of an earlier Currency Act of 1764, which made the colonists responsible for the entire domestic debt growing out of the Colonial Wars. Neither act was successful.

There was an instant and violent outcry by the colonists in response to the passage of all of these acts, but it was the Stamp Act that was most hotly resented. Patrick Henry in Virginia, and James Otis and Sam Adams in Massachusetts, were the most outspoken Americans in attacking the Stamp Act. Patrick Henry, while making a

21

speech in the Virginia House of Burgesses declaring that the British Parliament had absolutely no right to levy taxes against the American colonies, made an insulting remark about King George III.

He was interrupted by shouts of, "Treason! Treason!"

"I repeat," Patrick Henry replied, "Tarquin and Caesar each had his Brutus, Charles the First his Cromwell, and George the Third may profit by their example. If *this* be treason, make the most of it!"

Otis and Adams were equally outspoken, the latter saying, "If our commerce and trade are taxed, why not our lands? Why not the produce of our lands and everything we possess and make use of? If taxes are laid on us in any shape without our having legal representatives in Parliament, are we not reduced from free subjects to the miserable state of slaves?"

These men and many other early American patriots belonged to a group called the "Sons of Liberty." At the urging of the Sons of Liberty, a Stamp Act Congress was held in New York City during late October and early November in 1765. This resulted in a resolution stating that the colonists could not be taxed without their consent.

The colonists followed up their declaration with riots and a boycott of all English goods, refusing to buy anything but the barest of necessities from the mother country. This so alarmed British merchants that they appealed to Parliament, and the Stamp Act was repealed in 1766. Parliament nonetheless made it clear that, on behalf of England and the Crown, it still had the right to levy taxes on the colonies whenever it felt moved to do so.

Parliament felt moved to do so rather quickly. In 1767 Charles Townshend, Britain's chancellor of the exchequer, decided to make yet one more effort to raise money from the colonies. The Townshend Acts, which were readily passed by Parliament, placed import duties on certain goods that the colonists bought from England. These included such items as paper, glass, paint, lead—and tea.

Once again the colonists were roused to protest these new threats to America's liberties. It was Sam Adams who sent out a series of "Circular Letters," urging all of the colonies to unite and refuse to pay these illegal taxes. Great Britain retaliated by sending four regiments of redcoats to Boston in 1768 to maintain order, as well as to enforce the collection of the Townshend duties.

Sam Adams's appeal to his countrymen resulted in another boycott of British imports. This led, early in 1770, to a repeal of all of the Townshend duties except one—the tax on tea. Unfortunately, however, word of the repeal of most of the Townshend duties did not reach the colonies in time to prevent the clashes between the colonists and the British occupation troops that led to the Boston Massacre.

The Boston Massacre fanned the colonists' anger to white heat. A demand was made for the immediate trial of those guilty of firing into the crowd, and for the removal from Boston of all British troops. Some of the troops were removed, but far from all, and several weeks went by before those who had fired the shots were brought to trial. When the trial was announced, Sam Adams, as well as a number of his fellow citizens, were startled to learn that the redcoats were to be defended by a relative of Sam's, John Adams.

John Adams's agreement to defend the accused British soldiers did not mean that he was less patriotic than Sam Adams, or James Otis, or Patrick Henry, or any of the other Sons of Liberty. It simply meant that he had a built-in sense of fair play. These other American patriots —Sam Adams in particular—were fiery revolutionaries. John Adams was also a revolutionary, but he believed in the necessity for rules of law and justice in founding a sound society. And, in the case of the defendants in the Boston Massacre, he believed that the accused had a certain amount of right on their side. Most important, he felt that they were entitled to a fair trial.

The Adams family had come to America from England early in 1636, when the farmer Henry Adams, his wife, and their nine children settled on land at Wollaston, now Quincy, Massachusetts. Several generations of farmers later, young John Adams managed to escape the lot of his forebears by getting together enough money to enter Harvard College, presumably to study for the ministry. Instead, he turned to the study of law, and the first of several generations of great American public servants was born. Not only was he to become the second president of the United States after the Revolution, but he would also live long enough to see his son, John Quincy Adams, become president. A man of absolute integrity, John Adams's first political role during the pre-Revolutionary period was to argue the legality of the Stamp Act at the Stamp Act Congress. In opposition to the British, he argued its illegality. Now he was to be on the side of the British in defending the redcoats who had taken part in the Boston Massacre.

Sam Adams was a cousin of John Adams, but a distant one. His grandfather was a brother of John Adams's grandfather. He had been born in Boston, the son of a wealthy brewer, but he had been a revolutionary since his student days. The subject of his thesis for his master of arts degree at Harvard was, "Is it lawful to resist the supreme magistrate if the Commonwealth cannot otherwise be preserved?"

Although only distantly related, Sam Adams and John Adams had been closely associated ever since the first rumblings of the Revolution. Sam was constantly impatient with his cousin's insistence on a course of slow, orderly progress along the path toward American independence. While he strongly disagreed with John Adams's decision to defend the accused redcoats after the Boston Massacre, he supported his right to do so. Actually, Sam Adams was secretly glad the incident had occurred. (Some even said he had provoked it!) It made excellent fuel to feed the flames of rebellion.

The trial itself was an anticlimax. John Adams was assisted as defense counsel by Josiah Quincy, also a leading local lawyer. As a result of the efforts of the two defense lawyers, two of the soldiers received only minor punishment and the others were acquitted. Several witnesses testified that the redcoats had been driven to desperation by the taunts of the townspeople. Others said orders by Captain Thomas Preston, who was in charge of the guard, had been misinterpreted. Captain Preston had rushed to the scene early in the conflict. When he

Paul Revere's Ride (U.S. Office of War Information in the National Archives)

kept shouting, "Don't fire, don't fire, don't FIRE!" some thought this may have been misunderstood as a command to fire. Captain Preston was also exonerated.

Following the trial, interest in the controversy with Great Britain waned in the colonies. It was again Sam Adams who kept the issue of independence alive. In the course of doing so, he performed what was probably his greatest contribution to the American Revolution. In 1772, he organized what eventually became the revolutionary government in Massachusetts. This grew out of a so-called, Committee of Correspondence, which held its first meeting in Boston. Later there were similar committees throughout the colonies. These committees spread the spirit of unity among the colonies and kept the flame of rebellion burning. They actually were the first union of the colonies.

It was the strengthening of the Townshend tax on the import of tea that caused a final breach between the colonies and Great Britain. On May 10, 1773, Parliament passed British Prime Minister Lord North's Tea Act. This permitted the British East India Tea Company to sell its surplus tea more cheaply in the colonies than local merchants could sell the tea they imported.

Sam Adams immediately challenged this arrangement. He was strongly supported by local merchants. They were alarmed because they feared that, if the East India Tea Company gained a monopoly in selling tea in the colonies, it would be a simple matter for other companies to gain monopolies in the sale of other goods. Sam Adams managed to fan these fears into roaring flames of rebellion by acting as host at the Boston Tea Party.

Two

The Boston Tea
Party

The Boston Tea Party was a tea party such as the world had never known. To begin with, all the guests came dressed as Mohawk Indians.

Invitations to the exclusive affair were issued by Sam Adams at a meeting held in Boston's Old South Church, late on a dark December afternoon in 1773. Several thousand loyal Americans were present.

Adams informed those present that, even as he spoke, there were three British ships—the *Dartmouth*, the *Beaver*, and the *Eleanor*—docking at Griffin's wharf in Boston harbor.

"These ships are loaded with British East India Company tea," Adams said. "Should this tea be allowed to land?"

"No!" the audience roared.

Adams went on to explain that, despite the colonists' protests, the governor of Massachusetts, Thomas Hutchinson, stubbornly insisted that the tea *would* be landed. One final appeal was being made to Governor Hutchinson, Adams said. "Francis Rotch is now calling upon him to see if he will listen to reason."

At that moment Francis Rotch entered Old South Church and hurried up to the platform. He spoke to Adams in a whisper. There was a deathly silence in the room. Then Sam Adams announced solemnly, "The Governor has refused to meet our demands." He hesitated before going on. Finally he added, "There is now just one thing we can do to save our country."

There was a moment's silence, and then a war whoop rang out, followed by another and yet another. This was the signal for action already agreed upon by Sam Adams and his 150 carefully selected conspirators.

The meeting broke up immediately, and Sam Adams and his co-conspirators quickly made their way to Edes and Gill's print shop nearby. There they engaged in a curious activity. They looked as if they were making up for a part in a play. First they put on Indian clothing and headdresses. Then they took printer's ink and smeared it on their faces like war paint. Their makeup completed, Sam Adams's "Mohawk Indians," as they called themselves, sat silently waiting for night to fall.

When darkness at last came, the "Mohawks" crept out of the print shop and stealthily made their way toward Griffin's wharf. There they quickly climbed aboard the three British merchantmen. Silently the colonists disguised as Indians began to open up the chests of tea and

The Boston Tea Party (Minor Congressional Committee in the National Archives)

throw their contents into the harbor. Within a few hours the 342 chests were empty, and the raiders stole off quietly into the darkness to remove their makeup and return home.

As the wintry dawn broke over Boston harbor on December 17, 1773, tea could be seen floating atop the small waves that lapped at Griffin's wharf. This was the only evidence left of the previous night's tea party.

It took several months for the ripples of the news about the tea party to spread out from Boston harbor and to travel across the gray Atlantic to Great Britain;

but when the waves of information finally washed ashore in England, there was a loud demand for retaliation, and severe punitive action was taken against the colonists.

The British government passed the Coercive Acts— they were called the "Intolerable Acts" by the colonists —early in 1774. These included the closing of Boston harbor to all trade. The severity of the order startled even Sam Adams. Later Parliament suggested that, if the destroyed tea were paid for, all would be forgiven (its value would be $8,000 today). The Boston citizens, however, resolutely refused to be starved or bribed into submission. They received strong support from citizens throughout the colonies. Money and food—sheep, cattle, grain, flour, and potatoes—were sent to Boston with no requests for payment.

This spirit of unity led to a convention of the colonies to consider a plan of action against the mother country. The First Continental Congress assembled in Philadelphia in September, 1774, and lasted until late October. At this meeting a Declaration of Rights, or Declaration of Resolves, was written by John Adams. It was not a Declaration of Independence but simply a document that stated the colonists' grievances against the British government. If the British did not do something about remedying these grievances, the colonists agreed to hold another session of the Continental Congress to take further action.

During the next several months there were attempts on both sides of the Atlantic to narrow the widening breach between Britain and her colonies, but these efforts were of little avail. The Americans, goaded on by Sam Adams, became more and more defiant. Adams was now aided by his good friend, another member of the Sons of Liberty, John Hancock, who openly preached revolt. And in the south, Patrick Henry once again rose up in the Virginia House of Burgesses with a fiery and memorable speech. This time he declared:

"Gentlemen may cry peace! peace! but there *is* no peace! The war is actually begun! The next gale that sweeps down from the North will bring to our ears the clash of resounding arms! Our brethren are already in the field. Is life so dear, or peace so sweet, as to be purchased at the price of chains and slavery? Forbid it,

Patrick Henry demands "Liberty or Death" (Minor Congressional Committee in the National Archives)

Almighty God! I know not what course others may take, but as for me, give me liberty, or give me death!"

Soon the British military governor of Massachusetts, General Thomas Gage, received orders from England to arrest Sam Adams and John Hancock and send them to England for trial as rebels. Shortly after he received these orders, Gage learned that there were stores of ammunition—about 100 barrels of powder—and cannon at Concord, some eighteen miles from Boston, and that Adams and Hancock were staying in nearby Lexington. On the night of April 18, 1775, the British set out to capture the two rebel leaders and to destroy the military stores. Two other Sons of Liberty, Paul Revere and William Dawes, immediately set out on horseback to warn Adams and Hancock that the British were coming. Adams and Hancock were staying at the Reverend Jonas Clark's in Lexington. They received the warning in time and managed to remain hidden.

The next morning, a force of some two hundred redcoats, led by Major John Pitcairn of the Royal Marines, arrived in Lexington. There they encountered some 38 "Minutemen," as the rebel patriot soldiers called themselves, scattered in loose battle formation across the village green. (Altogether there were about 7,500 Minutemen throughout New England; they were well trained and well armed.)

Pitcairn ordered Captain John Parker, commander of the Lexington Minutemen, to disperse his forces. Parker refused to do so, saying to his men, "Don't fire unless fired upon, but if they mean to have a war, let it begin here."

Suddenly a single shot was fired. No one knew who

fired this first shot, but a moment later the British were firing furiously at will. Only about eight Minutemen managed to return this opening fusillade. Then, as quickly as it had begun, all firing ceased. Eight dead and nine wounded patriots lay sprawled across Lexington green. One British soldier was wounded in the leg, and Major Pitcairn's horse was hit in the flank.

When Sam Adams heard the rattle of muskets from the village, he is said to have declared, "Oh, what a glorious morning!"

The redcoats now marched on to Concord, the skirmish at Lexington having delayed them only fifteen minutes. At Concord they were able to destroy some of the military stores—gunpowder and a number of buried cannon. Here, too, there was a brief skirmish. In this fight, at the North Bridge over the Concord River, the British fired first, killing two men. In response the Minutemen fired "the shot heard round the world," killing three redcoats and wounding nine. The deadly exchange lasted perhaps five minutes.

The British then began their return march to Boston. This retreat turned into one of the costliest ever suffered by British regulars. All along the route, the redcoats had to run a gauntlet of fire laid down by American patriots hidden behind trees and rocks and stone fences. American farmers from the surrounding countryside, who had heard the musket fire at both Lexington and Concord, put aside their farm tools, picked up their muskets, and set out for the scene of action. Not only did they lie in wait for the British column as it approached their hiding places along the trail, but they also attacked the column from the rear after it had gone by. In fact, the most

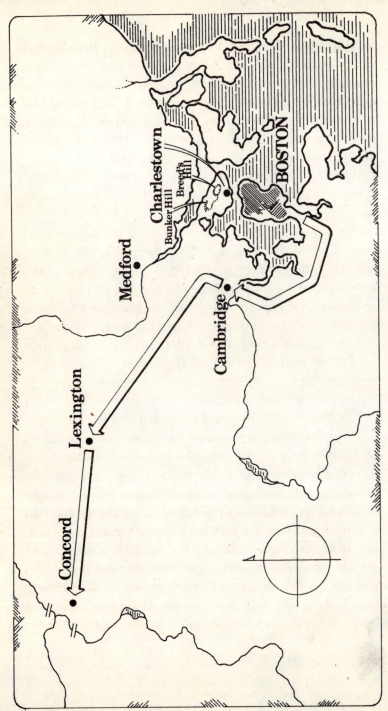

Route taken from Boston to Concord

Retreat from Concord (Fine Arts Commission in the National Archives)

endangered part of the column proved to be that at the rear.

Against this completely unorthodox, "dirty" style of fighting—European soldiers were schooled in fighting each other at close quarters, face-to-face in the open—the redcoats at first displayed remarkable courage. Nearing Lexington, however, discipline broke down, and they began to bolt and run. It was at this point that they were met by the vanguard of some 1,500 relief troops sent out by General Gage from Boston. Here a handful of teen-

37

aged redcoat officers displayed the cool courage that had made the British army famous throughout the world. They raced into the thick of the fighting at the rear of the column and calmly stood their ground, forcing the withdrawing regulars to slow their retreat, and reestablishing iron discipline.

One of the problems facing the British regulars, as they ran the gauntlet of embattled farmers, was that they had been trained to kneel and reload after each round was fired from their muskets. This took from fifteen to twenty seconds, during which time the redcoats were perfectly stationary targets.* The Americans continued to remain hidden behind trees or other obstructions as

*The smoothbore, flintlock musket was the common weapon of the British regulars. Called "Brown Bess," it weighed about fourteen pounds. The barrel was more than forty inches long and about three-quarters of an inch in diameter. A fourteen-inch bayonet could be fixed to the barrel.

Cartridges were carried in a container called a *cartouche* box worn at the waist. Cartridges were made of paper, and each contained a lead ball and loose black powder. To load the musket one end of the cartridge was first bitten off. Then a small amount of powder was poured into the flashpan, where it would be ignited by a piece of flint when the musket's trigger was pulled. The remaining powder was poured down the barrel, followed by the bullet. A ramrod was used to ram tight the barrel's contents.

Most soldiers could load and fire at least three rounds a minute. Experts could fire as many as six.

The American patriots also used smoothbore muskets, although some fired the more accurate Pennsylvania rifle. Later in the war the patriots used an improved French musket called the Charleville, which became the standard weapon of the Continental army.

they reloaded. If they were in the open, they reloaded while sprawled full length upon the ground.

The heavily reinforced British column finally made its way back to Charlestown and Boston, but the brief foray had been a disaster. Gage's losses were 274 killed and wounded, while the colonists had 88 men killed and wounded. According to British records, the last colonist killed was an unnamed black man.

The American Revolution had now begun. The Americans would undergo their next test of fire at Bunker Hill.

Three

The Siege of Boston

Once the British were back in Boston, the Americans decided to lay siege to the city, keeping Gage's garrison bottled up on the peninsula. Thousands of armed patriots from all over New England swarmed into Cambridge and Roxbury. Soon Boston was ringed by a half-circle of earthwork fortifications that the militiamen erected in preparation for the siege. At night, the citizens and redcoats inside the city could see the circle of surrounding campfires on the hills. Neither the Americans nor the British made any attempt to alter this situation for two months. They did so at the Battle of Bunker Hill on June 17, 1775.

The major action in the Battle of Bunker Hill actually took place on nearby Breed's Hill. The patriots decided to fortify Breed's Hill rather than Bunker Hill because the former was closer to Boston. The selection of this site proved to be a serious mistake on the part of the Americans.

Before the Battle of Bunker Hill took place, however, the Second Continental Congress was held in Philadelphia, beginning on May 10. Here it was recommended that a Continental army be formed. John Hancock, president of the Congress, expected to be named commander in chief of this army. He was bitterly disappointed when a forty-three-year-old colonel in the Virginia militia, George Washington, was given this appointment, two days before the Battle of Bunker Hill. A veteran leader of campaigns against the French in the Colonial Wars, Washington was nominated as commander of the Continental army by John Adams, and his nomination was seconded by Sam Adams. Washington did not assume command until July 3, so he took no part in the Battle of Bunker Hill.

Meanwhile, Gage's besieged British garrison was reinforced by 2,700 additional troops sent from Great Britain. (Boston harbor was, of course, open to the British.) Gage was given personal support also, with the arrival from England of a trio of top British Generals: John Burgoyne, Henry Clinton, and William Howe. All three were seasoned combat veterans.

The most colorful of this trio was "Gentleman Johnny" Burgoyne. Not only was Gentleman Johnny a military man with a fine reputation as a cavalry commander, but he was also a member of Parliament and a playwright.

Clinton had the least attractive personality of the

three. A fair-haired, quiet little man, he had been an officer at thirteen and was still boyish-looking in his late thirties. He had a habit of constantly mumbling complaints about lack of judgment and ability on the part of his superiors. His mumbled complaints were to be heard virtually throughout the course of the Revolution.

A tall, well-built man, General Howe was often said to resemble George Washington in appearance and manner. The dark-visaged Howe's reputation had been established during the French and Indian War at Quebec, where he and his men had scaled the city's steep cliffs and, with General James Wolfe, had stormed to victory against the French on the Plains of Abraham. His oldest brother, General George Howe, had been killed at Ticonderoga in 1758 in the Colonial Wars. Massachusetts citizens later contributed funds for a monument to be erected to George Howe in Westminster Abbey. Another older brother, Richard "Black Dick" Howe, was an Admiral in the Royal Navy. He would soon be stationed in American waters. Because of the honor paid their eldest brother George by the Americans, neither General William Howe nor Admiral Richard Howe wanted to fight against the patriots in the Revolution. They had agreed to come to America only when ordered to do so by the king.

General Clinton's first major complaint against his superior officer, General Gage, was that Gage seemed reluctant to take any action. Clinton could readily see that at least two high points above the city—Dorchester Heights in Roxbury to the south and Bunker Hill in Charlestown to the north—should be seized by the British. If the Americans seized these heights and installed cannon on them, it would be impossible for the British to withstand the resulting bombardment and remain in the city.

Clinton also learned that early in May, shortly before he and Generals Burgoyne and Howe had arrived, a combined force of colonial troops led by Colonels Ethan Allen and Benedict Arnold had captured the British-held Fort Ticonderoga at the foot of Lake Champlain. Fort Ticonderoga was often called the "Gibraltar of North America." In many ways it was actually the key to the North American continent because it offered easy access to Canada by way of Lake Champlain, Lake George, and the St. Lawrence River. Its possession had been fiercely contested all during the Colonial Wars. Most important of all was the fact that some fifty-nine cannon and numerous other weapons in excellent condition had been captured by Allen, Arnold, and Allen's "Green Mountain Boys" in their recent expedition. These invaluable guns would not arrive in the Boston area for some months, but the Americans had other weapons immediately available.

Consequently, it now became a question of which side would first seize and fortify the heights that dominated the Boston peninsula both to the north and to the south.

The day dawned bright, clear, and hot.

Suddenly, the quiet dawn was shattered by the sounds of gunfire from the several British warships anchored in Boston harbor. Captain Thomas Bishop, aboard H.M.S. *Lively,* had been awakened by a lookout who had seen earthworks that had been built on top of Breed's Hill by the Americans during the night. Bishop had immediately

Capture of Fort Ticonderoga. When Ethan Allen, accompanied by Benedict Arnold (not shown), took over Fort Ticonderoga, Allen was reported to have demanded the Fort's surrender, "In the name of the Great Jehovah and the Continental Congress." However, Arnold reported that what Allen actually said to the British Commander was, "You damned old rat, come out!" (Chicago Historical Society)

ordered his gunners to open fire on the earthwork redoubt, and soon every gun in the small British fleet had joined in.

General Artemas Ward of Massachusetts, who was in charge of the 5,000 provincial militiamen outside Boston, had received word on June 13 that the British planned to occupy Bunker Hill on June 18. Although he was extremely cautious by nature, Ward acted decisively on this occasion. He ordered Colonel William Prescott, also of Massachusetts, to move out on the evening of June 16 with about 1,000 men and fortify Bunker Hill. Ward decided to hold back the rest of his troops to defend Cambridge.

Although he felt his lifework to be that of a farmer, William Prescott seemed to be a natural-born military commander. As a teen-ager he had fought valiantly in the Colonial Wars and had been offered a commission in the regular British army. He had refused the commission in favor of returning to his farm, but when the Minutemen were formed he had been elected a colonel in his local detachment. No better man could have been chosen to lead the rebels on this historic occasion.

As they marched toward the Charlestown peninsula and Bunker Hill on the night of June 16, Prescott and his Massachusetts Provincial Army were joined by General Israel Putnam and Colonel Nathanael Greene, accompanied by several hundred Connecticut and Rhode Island troops.

General Putnam—always called "Old Put"—was a veteran Indian fighter. Although he was almost sixty years of age, Old Put was still a commanding figure. Built like a bear and with a voice like a bull, he completely dominated friend and foe alike with the sheer force of his personality. He had fought beside General George Howe when Howe had been killed at Ticonderoga, had been a prisoner of both the Indians and the French, and had narrowly escaped death a half a dozen times—including once when he had almost been burned at the stake.

Putnam outranked Prescott, but he generously declined to assume command of the Bunker Hill force. Nevertheless, his powerful personality undoubtedly played a part in the decision to fortify Breed's Hill rather than Bunker Hill. Prescott actually announced this decision after a discussion with Old Put and Colonel Richard Gridley, an engineering officer.

Gridley then marked out an area for the building of the fort or redoubt, a forty-yard square with a breastwork facing the enemy. The men were ordered to dig out a deep trench in this area, throwing up the earth for the breastwork. They set to work with shovels and pickaxes, digging up the raw, red clay with astonishing speed. It was a hot and difficult task, and there was little or no water available to drink. Nevertheless, the men kept at it, and by dawn the construction was almost completed.

Dawn also revealed that the redoubt should have been built atop nearby Bunker Hill, which was higher than Breed's Hill. If the British succeeded in occupying Bunker Hill, they could fire down on Prescott's forces on Breed's Hill with devastating effect.

It was at this point that the British aboard the warships in the harbor spotted the redoubt and opened fire on it.

Despite the heavy cannon fire, Prescott drove his men on with their work. At his left, there was a stone and rail fence that led down to a beach at the water's edge. This he had reinforced with earth and more stones by the men who were to be stationed behind it. His right flank, he trusted, would be somewhat protected by Charlestown.

As the British firing continued, Old Put was back on

Bunker Hill with a small detachment attempting to fortify it to some degree in case of a retreat. Twice, Prescott had Putnam ride back across Charlestown neck to request reinforcements from Artemas Ward. Ward finally granted the request, sending two New Hampshire regiments to assist Prescott.

Prescott's forces were then also joined by Dr. Robert Warren, a newly promoted general officer who, like Old Put, said he was just a volunteer and refused to take over command from Prescott. Dr. Warren was a Boston physician who had given up his medical practice to fight with the colonists against the British. It was Warren who had sent out Paul Revere and William Dawes to alert the countryside that the British were marching on Lexington and Concord. He had personally been with the Minutemen at those two fatal meeting places, and had helped harass the British back along the bloody gauntlet to Charlestown and Boston.

The total American force at Breed's Hill and Bunker Hill at that point numbered about 1,600 men.

As soon as he saw that the rebels had dug in on Breed's Hill, British General Clinton suggested that troops be sent to the rear of the enemy at Charlestown neck. There they could climb Bunker Hill and fire down on the enemy below. Gage rejected this suggestion. He was supported by Burgoyne and Howe.

Howe, in particular, objected to mounting any kind of elaborate attack against the nonprofessional American militia, which he regarded as a mere rabble in arms. He still regretted having to fight against the Americans, but he did not regard them highly as fighting men. Farmers and merchants, yes; soldiers, no. As a proud professional

Breed's Hill and Bunker Hill

soldier, Howe thought that he and his fellow professionals should simply clear out this rabble quickly, directly,
and with as little fuss as possible. Howe's attitude resulted in the decision to mount a direct frontal assault on
Breed's Hill.

Howe, who was placed in immediate charge of the
attacking forces, went about leisurely giving orders for
the dispersal of his approximately 2,400 men. He regarded the attack as a formal military set piece with the
outcome a foregone conclusion.

Meanwhile, the citizens of Boston regarded the coming battle not merely as a set piece but as a showpiece.
Thousands thronged the high ground in Charlestown
and the roofs of houses on the north side of Boston, and
watched the battle unfold before them like a pageant.
Atop Penn's Hill in nearby Braintree, John Adams's wife,
Abigail, stood holding the hand of their eight-year-old
son, John Quincy Adams, who was to be the sixth president of the United States.

Early in the afternoon, the spectators saw two dozen
large rowboats leave the wharves at Boston and move
across the channel toward Morton's Point on Charlestown peninsula, near Breed's Hill. Despite the heat of
the day, each British regular wore a woolen uniform and
carried a full field pack that weighed well over 100
pounds. The trip was repeated several times before all of
the redcoats, including a number of reserves, had
landed. The reserves were a battalion of marines led by
Major Pitcairn, who had led the Lexington-Concord redcoat forces.

Howe's plan was simple. He would personally lead the
infantry and grenadiers in an attack on the stone and rail

49

fence. A flanking force would work its way up from the beach. Once the rail-fence defensive position was breached by Howe's forces at the front and the flanking force from the side, the combined attackers could get in behind the redoubt. The other half of the British troops would make a frontal attack straight up Breed's Hill, in the face of the enemy lying behind the breastwork in the redoubt.

Howe was as brave as he was unimaginative. "I will not ask a single one of you," he told his men just before the battle, "to go anywhere I would not go first." He was as good as his word.

Before the infantry attack began, Howe ordered that a barrage be put down on the enemy from his ten six-pound cannon. However, his cannon had been supplied with the wrong-sized shot and were useless. Later in the day this fault was remedied.

In the redoubt and behind the rail fence, the rebels lay quietly waiting, their muskets and rifles placed on firm resting points to steady each marksman's aim. Unknown to the British, the Americans had arranged that only their best marksmen would be firing. And, for each marksman, two men had been selected to load the empty muskets or rifles, so as to avoid delay between volleys.

As the British drums began to signal the attack, the redcoats moved out in long, even lines, their uniforms bright in the hot sunlight. They looked as if they were marching in a dress parade. More than one provincial soldier thought the enemy looked too handsome to shoot. But they knew there was no choice.

Slowly, steadily, the flanking redcoats moved up from

the beach while the front force moved through the long, thick grass toward the rail fence.

Again and again, Colonel Prescott cautioned his men against firing too soon. When they did begin to fire, they had been told, they were to aim at the point where the redcoats' white, pipe-clayed belts crisscrossed on their chests. They had also been told to fire at the officers first. Prescott may also have said, "Don't fire until you see the whites of their eyes." If he did, he was repeating a remark made by Prince Charles of Prussia in a European battle more than a quarter of a century earlier.

Up the slope the long lines of doomed redcoats went, firing an occasional volley although they also had been told not to fire too soon, but rather to take the enemy's position with a bayonet charge.

The redcoats coming up from the beach received the first volleys, but not until they were fifty feet away from the rebels, looking not at all like toy soldiers now but like the larger-than-life, professional British soldiers they were, long-schooled experts at their military trade—and their trade was dealing in sudden death.

"Fire!"

Colonel Prescott's command was drowned out by the first murderous volley from patriot guns. Down went dozens of advancing redcoats. Others continued to advance. A second volley, and fifty more British officers and men fell in the blood-stained grass. The shattered lines wavered. A third volley, and the remaining redcoats broke and ran. As they did so, the rebels stood and cheered. The first attack had failed.

Howe immediately rallied his men for a second attack,

a direct one on the rail fence. If successful, it would still enable him to get in behind the redoubt. The disciplined redcoats quickly re-formed into row upon row of determined attackers, bent on avenging their comrades who had just fallen around them, and also those who had fallen on the way back from Lexington and Concord.

Once again the drums sounded, rattling out their grim signal to advance, and once again the British moved forward. Still wearing their unbearably heavy field packs, the redcoats came on relentlessly. Leading them was General Howe.

Again the patriots waited until the British were only a few steps away. So close were the redcoats that they could see the grim, feverish-eyed faces of the rebels between the rails in the fence.

"Fire!"

Again the command was given, and again the British went down in windrows.

A second volley sounded, and Howe looked around him to see that he was standing alone, his uniform spattered with blood from those who had gone down around him. A strange, deathly wind seemed to be blowing, and a sudden awesome silence filled the day.

"At that moment," Howe said afterward, "I had a feeling I had never known before."

It was a feeling that was to stay with him for the remainder of the Revolution, for never again was he to be the iron-willed, decisive general he had been before. Something was drained from his military spirit on that dreadful day.

Nevertheless, Howe rallied his remaining men and prepared for a third attack.

Back in Boston, watching the attack through field glasses, were Generals Gage, Burgoyne, and Clinton. Before the battle it had not been felt that their presence would be needed. Now it was too late for their presence to be of any use. The three prayed that General Howe would not make a third attempt to take Breed's Hill. But they knew he must.

This time Howe told his men to remove their packs. As the redcoats re-formed for a third attack—directly on the redoubt this time—the rebels behind the breastwork felt their first feeling of dismay. They too had lost men, though only a handful compared with the British, but their most serious problem was a lack of powder. What was left was distributed equally among the defenders, but they knew it was not enough to last.

The British again came forward, this time in a line of skirmishers with large gaps between each man. When a man fell, another moved up from the rear to replace him. They moved at a dead run, with shouts of encouragement to one another that could be heard back in Boston. As they neared the breastwork, a volley sounded, and another, and then there was silence. The rebel powder was exhausted.

Leaping across the parapet, the British attacked with bayonets. The patriots fought back, using their muskets as clubs, rocks, and even their fists. Here the British Major Pitcairn died, as did Dr. Warren.

Colonel Prescott lived to lead his men in a hasty but well-executed retreat back to Bunker Hill, where General Putnam's men provided covering fire. But their ammunition was also low, and soon all of the patriot forces were in a general retreat from the Charlestown peninsula.

Many critics felt that if Howe had followed up this victory at Breed's Hill by pursuing the rebel forces, he might have completely destroyed them at Cambridge. But the victory had been a hollow one, and Howe and his men had no taste for further fighting. British losses amounted to almost half of those engaged—226 killed and 828 wounded—at a time when most badly wounded men died. A high proportion of the casualties were officers.

Afterward General Clinton commented, "An expensive victory. Another like it would have ruined us."

American casualties were 140 killed and 271 wounded. Most of these casualties were suffered during the retreat.

Patriot Nathanael Greene's comment was, "I wish we would sell them another hill at the same price."

General Gage said, "These people show a spirit against us that they never showed against the French in the Colonial Wars. The loss we have sustained is greater than we can bear."

Neither side celebrated a victory after Bunker Hill, and neither side had actually won one, except perhaps the Americans in a moral sense. The British had displayed arrogant stupidity in not simply surrounding the Americans at Breed's Hill, where the patriots could have easily been left to starve. The Americans had been equally stupid in fortifying Breed's Hill rather than Bunker Hill. Nevertheless, they had proved to the world and most especially to the British that they were ready, willing, and able to stand and fight for their rights. And if they had not run out of ammunition . . . well, it was something interesting to speculate about.

Because the Battle of Breed's or Bunker Hill had been something of a stalemate, the war would now have to be decided by fighting in other theaters. The next battles were to take place in Canada to the north and the Carolinas to the south.

Four

Success in Boston;
Failure at Quebec

For almost a year after the Breed's Hill–Bunker Hill battle, the British made no move to break out of Boston or to evacuate the city by sea. British military commanders were afraid that if they tried to break out, every surrounding high point of ground might well turn into another Breed's Hill. And there were not enough ships to evacuate the redcoats.

This lack of shipping was a typical reason for the failure of British strategic plans all through the Revolution. British overall strategic plans were, from a military viewpoint, excellent. They included separating the troublemaking New England colonies from the other colonies; isolating the central colonies and thus cutting off much of the rebels' food supplies; controlling the south-

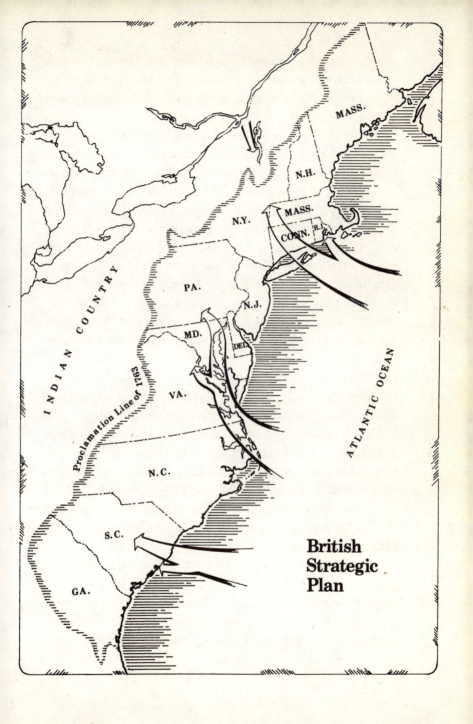

British
Strategic
Plan

ern colonies by seizing Charleston and Georgetown in South Carolina; and blockading the entire east coast from north to south, thus cutting off both supplies and weapons from abroad.

The British government in London failed to carry out fully any of these plans. Parliament also failed to provide sufficient troops and shipping. The war was not popular in England, so enlistments declined. The British partially met this need for men by hiring some 30,000 troops from Germany. Because many of these mercenary soldiers came from the German state of Hesse-Cassel, they were called *Hessians.* Even these hired troops did not give the British a sufficient force to maintain control of an invaded area by occupying it. And the Americans continued to fight what was then a novel kind of guerrilla warfare that made larger and larger British forces essential. Finally, the long, irregular east coast and the activities of American privateers—armed, private vessels authorized to attack the British merchant and warships—made a successful blockade virtually impossible.

Morale among the occupying redcoats in Boston was extremely low during the rest of 1775 and the winter of 1776. They had little to do to keep them busy, and disease—mainly smallpox and scurvy—as well as lack of food and fuel plagued them. In addition, they continued to lack faith in their leaders after the debacle of Breed's Hill.

In the autumn of 1775, General Gage was relieved of his command and recalled to England. In his place two men were named to head military operations in North America. The governor of Canada, Sir Guy Carleton, was placed in command of the redcoats in Canada, and

General William Howe took over complete command of the redcoats in the American colonies.

Meanwhile, General George Washington went about recruiting men for the Continental army. He now began to face a problem that was to plague him throughout the course of the war. The troops were all volunteers whose enlistments ran out after a certain period of time. He was faced immediately with the prospect of losing half of his volunteer army at the end of 1775. Furthermore, many of the colonies—especially those in the south—were willing to field individual colonial armies but were not very much interested in offering troops to the Continental army. Washington and his staff officers did their best to combat this troublesome situation, but gradually they saw their army begin to wither away.

Washington also concentrated on forcing the British to leave Boston. To accomplish this, cannon were needed to fortify a nearby hill, Dorchester Heights, so that the city could be made untenable. The required cannon turned out to be those captured at Ticonderoga by Colonels Benedict Arnold and Ethan Allen and his Green Mountain Boys, shortly before the Battle of Breed's Hill.

"No trouble or expense must be spared to get those cannon to Boston," George Washington said.

The man Washington chose to do the job was Henry Knox, a former Boston bookstore owner and amateur artillery expert, who had taught himself the artilleryman's trade by reading books on the subject. Professional soldiers were always amazed at the depth of Knox's military knowledge. He was a huge, red-faced man more than six feet tall and weighing almost 300 pounds. As brave as he was big, he would soon become artillery commander of the Continental army and, after the Revolution, Washington's first secretary of war.

All of Knox's driving courage was needed to lead his "royal train of artillery," as he called it, across the wintry wastes from Fort Ticonderoga to Boston. The distance covered was 300 miles, and the fifty-nine heavy cannon plus mortars and other weapons had to be hauled on ox-drawn sledges across steep hills covered with ice and snow. The heroic task took from early December, 1775, to late February, 1776. When it was accomplished, however, the fate of the British in Boston was sealed.

Washington hurriedly built fortifications on Dorchester Heights and installed the cannon. Exactly as they had before the Battle of Breed's Hill, the British in Boston awakened one morning to see the new fortifications, this time complete with menacing cannon, looming over them.

Disgustedly, Howe said, "The rebels have done more in one night than my whole army could have done in months."

Howe gave some thought to attempting a breakout from the city, but finally he decided to evacuate it instead, as he now had a few additional troop transports available. He ordered these and the other ships in the harbor to be filled with British troops. On March 16, 1776, he and his small army sailed from Boston harbor to Halifax, Nova Scotia, where there was a British naval base.

The next day the rebel forces, led by General Israel Old Put Putnam, triumphantly occupied the city. Washington entered Boston on March 18. He did not request a victory celebration; instead he asked that a memorial service of thanksgiving be held.

Washington knew that it was far too early to celebrate a victory. Elsewhere the war had been going badly for the Americans, especially at Quebec, in Canada, which had been under siege for months.

Several weeks after they and their men had captured Fort Ticonderoga on May 10, 1775, Colonels Allen and Arnold had volunteered to lead an expedition into Canada to prevent the British from using Canadian bases. Several members of the Continental Congress, however, thought that Canada could be talked into coming into the war on the side of the American colonies as a "fourteenth colony." When this effort failed it was decided that Canada must be conquered—or at least neutralized—but that neither Allen nor Arnold should lead the expedition to accomplish this task. Instead the job was given to another rebel leader, General Philip Schuyler. This angered both Allen and Arnold, two of the most colorful and contradictory men in the American Revolution.

A native of Connecticut, Ethan Allen had served with distinction in the French and Indian War at Fort William Henry. Shortly before the Revolution, he had moved to what was known as the "New Hampshire Grants" (today's Vermont), an area claimed, under their colonial grants, by both New York and New Hampshire. As New Hampshire claimants, Allen and his Green Mountain Boys—a force of volunteer fighters—warred against the rival New Yorkers. When the Revolution began, Allen's Green Mountain Boys followed him into battle against the British. Much later in the war, Allen was made a general by the Hampshire Grant (Vermont) settlers, and it was said that Allen plotted with the British to create a separate province out of Vermont. For this he was to be accused of treason—a questionable charge that was finally suspended.

Benedict Arnold was also a native of Connecticut, but he had received his temporary officer's commission from Massachusetts. He had been a successful merchant and trader immediately before the Revolution, following limited service as a fourteen-year-old volunteer in the Colonial Wars. A well-built, rather stocky man, Arnold was ambitious and restless to the point of recklessness.

Immediately after Arnold and Allen had captured Ticonderoga, Arnold had proceeded to occupy Crown Point. There he had received word that he was to be succeeded in command by an as yet unnamed officer in the regular Massachusetts Militia. This made Arnold furious to the point of insubordination. After being relieved of his command, Arnold was also accused of mishandling funds entrusted to him by Massachusetts, a charge that was finally dropped. Although he was a man of great courage and was one of the early heroes of the American forces in the Revolution, Arnold's arrogance and egotism eventually led him to commit treason. Some of his fellow officers—perhaps out of jealousy—said that Arnold "would do anything for money." If that was true, this attitude may have helped lead him to his eventual downfall.

Fortunately, Philip Schuyler, the man chosen to lead the expedition against Canada, had an able second in command, since Schuyler himself seemed completely lacking in dash and daring. Schuyler's aide was General

Richard Montgomery, a former British officer who had fought in the Colonial Wars and then married an American woman and settled in the colonies. He urged Schuyler to move against Montreal as soon as possible. Montgomery's sense of urgency was prompted by a letter sent to Ticonderoga by John Brown, an American woodsman and a close friend of the Indians in the area. Brown warned the American commander that Sir Guy Carleton was preparing to sweep south on Lake Champlain and recapture Fort Ticonderoga.

When Schuyler continued to delay, Montgomery set off north on Lake Champlain from Crown Point in late August, 1775, with about 1,000 Americans. They were joined at the last minute by Ethan Allen, who had had second thoughts about the coming engagement. No matter who was leading it, one thing Allen dearly loved was a fight.

Montgomery laid siege to the British fort of St. John's on the Richelieu River, the water exit from Champlain, sending Allen and 100 of his men around the flank toward Montreal. Here Allen was suddenly surrounded by a large force of Canadians and Indians sent out by Sir Guy Carleton. Allen and his men fought gallantly, but all were finally killed or captured. Allen was among those taken prisoner.

Montgomery continued his siege of St. John's until the fort surrendered on November 3. Less than two weeks later, he also occupied Montreal, but not before Carleton, disguised as a fisherman, had escaped and made his way toward Quebec. (Ethan Allen was held a prisoner in England until October, 1776, when he was returned to America, on parole, in an exchange of prisoners. His

General Charles Cornwallis (National Portrait Gallery, London)

questionable dealings with the British to make Vermont a British province began in 1780.)

Shortly after the fall of Montreal, Montgomery learned that an American force was standing outside Quebec and was calling upon Montgomery for reinforcements. The leader of this force was Benedict Arnold. Montgomery immediately hurried to join Arnold before the Canadian citadel.

It had been George Washington's decision to send Arnold against Quebec. Washington had long admired Arnold, whom he had known since Arnold was a teenager fighting in the French and Indian War. Now, to appease the dashing hero of Ticonderoga, he had placed him in charge of this diversionary attack that he hoped would draw British attention away from Montgomery's move down the St. Lawrence.

With a force of 1,000 volunteers, Arnold had left Cambridge in mid-September, 1775. The expedition was to be one of the most epic in American military history. Their 180-mile journey was to take them up Maine's Kennebec River and down the Chaudière River in Canada to the St. Lawrence. They traveled in whale boats, or bateaux. The boats had been badly built, and many of them leaked and were swamped or fell apart in the swift, rapids-filled waters. A number of men were lost when the whale boats smashed against rocks and fallen trees. Long portages up steep hills were frequent. To make their way through one long series of rapids Arnold and his remaining men had to wade for almost 200 miles. Here, too, men were lost. Others died as winter descended and food ran out. Those who survived did so by eating soap, candles, grease, and boiled leather clothing and equipment. Desertions also depleted the dwindling force, but Arnold drove his men on. Finally, in early November, the expedition, reduced to fewer than 600 skeletonlike men, arrived before Quebec. The journey had been planned to take three weeks. It had taken twice that long to cover what proved to be more than 350 miles.

Leaving many of his troops behind him in Montreal, Montgomery and 300 men joined Arnold in early December at Pointe aux Trembles above Quebec. While waiting for Montgomery, the impatient Arnold had already led his men up the steep cliffs and onto the Plains of Abraham, just as General Wolfe had done at the close of the Colonial Wars. Unlike Wolfe, however, Arnold and his men failed to defeat the enemy garrison there; instead they had been driven off. They were recovering from this setback when Montgomery and his meager band of reinforcements arrived.

Meanwhile, the Quebec garrison under Sir Guy Carleton had been reinforced by 2,000 men.

Arnold and Montgomery were faced with an almost impossible situation. Their forces were scarcely large enough to attack the citadel city, and yet they could not maintain a siege through the remainder of the winter, since they had no siege guns. Further, they were short of food, and smallpox and scurvy had broken out. Their decision was to attack, mainly because the period of enlistment for many of their men would end with the coming of the new year.

The attack was launched in the middle of a blinding snowstorm on the night of December 30, 1775. The results were a foregone conclusion. Montgomery was killed almost immediately, and his men's morale died with him. Arnold was badly wounded in the leg. The rebel forces were either taken prisoner or escaped in great disorder.

The escaping forces did manage to take Arnold with them, and a camp and hospital were established not far from Quebec at St. Roch. Here, from his hospital bed, Arnold directed his troops to lay siege to Quebec—at least until spring when he knew the British would receive their annual reinforcements from Great Britain. Some cannon were obtained from Montgomery's remaining forces at Montreal, and a desultory fire was laid down for some weeks. The British refused to venture outside the city, so Arnold's siege was allowed to continue by the enemy's failure to take any action. No further attempts were made by the rebels to attack Quebec. As a matter of fact, no further attempts were made against Canada during the remainder of the war.

Early in May, Washington sent General John Thomas to Montreal. His orders were to cover a retreat by Arnold's forces. Thomas, however, died of smallpox. A physician in civilian life, Thomas had heard of Edward Jenner's recent experiments with smallpox vaccinations; but, like most people of his day, he had refused to be inoculated against the disease. His post was taken by General John Sullivan. Sullivan and his reinforcements managed to cover Arnold's evacuation to Montreal, and from there back down Lake Champlain to Fort Ticonderoga. They arrived in July, 1776.

For an unexplained reason, Sir Guy Carleton made no immediate attempt against Fort Ticonderoga, which he could easily have taken. Nevertheless, the St. Lawrence–Lake Champlain–Hudson River route now lay wide open to the British, like an arrow pointed at the heart of New York and the rest of the northern colonies.

Fortunately, the rebels had been faring somewhat better against the British in the southern colonies.

Five

A Day in July

Throughout the Revolution there were many Americans who remained loyal to Great Britain and the Crown. These Loyalists, or Tories, were hated by the American patriots, whom they almost equalled in numbers. Even the apparently mild-mannered George Washington said more than once that all Tory leaders should be hanged as examples. Other patriots contented themselves with confiscating Tory homes and businesses, chasing the owners through the streets, and hurling taunts, eggs, and rocks at them. Some Tories were tarred and feathered and driven out of town. Others were fined and imprisoned if they refused to curse the king and swear loyalty to the patriot cause.

Several royal governors were jailed or forced to flee

America and return to England or take refuge with the redcoat army. Among these was the governor of Virginia, Lord Dunmore, who refused to leave without striking back at the rebels. Assembling a fleet in Chesapeake Bay and rallying Tories, redcoats, and escaped Negro slaves to his cause, he staged several raids on the Virginia coast. But he and his raiders were met and defeated outside Norfolk on December 11, 1775. Dunmore managed to board a ship and flee to New York City, where, the following summer he joined the main British army. Dunmore's futile but gallant stand encouraged many American Tories in their opposition to the rebels.

The British Parliament, well aware of this hard core of Loyalists within the colonies, sought to take advantage of the situation by encouraging the Tories to stand and fight against the patriots. Lord George Germain, named by King George III as secretary of state for the American colonies, was one of the strongest believers in a Tory uprising. To back his belief, Germain sponsored a British expedition against America's southern colonies where the Tories were especially numerous. Germain believed that as soon as this southern expedition appeared on the scene, a mass Tory uprising would occur. The expedition from England was to be led by General Charles Cornwallis and Admiral Peter Parker. They were to be met, off the North Carolina coast, by a seaborne detachment of General Howe's troops under the command of General Henry Clinton. The rendezvous was scheduled for early in 1776, but due to severe storms it did not take place until the spring.

Meanwhile, in February, North Carolina's royal governor, Josiah Martin, rallied 1,500 Tories to rise up against

BALTIMORE

POTOMAC RIVER

FREDERICKSBURG

CHARLOTTESVILLE

RICHMOND
WILLIAMSBURG
YORKTOWN
PETERSBURG
PORTSMOUTH

Roanoke River

HILLSBORO

GUILFORD

Cape Fear River

Kings Mt.
CHARLOTTE

Moore's
Creek
Bridge

Cowpens

Waxhaws

WILMINGTON

Santee River

CAMDEN

Savanna River

GEORGETOWN
Fort Watson
Orangeburg
Eutaw Springs

AUGUSTA

CHARLESTON

Stono Ferry

Port Royal Island

PURRYSBURG

SAVANNAH

SUNBURY

The
Southern
Theater
of
War

the rebels and drive them into the sea. Martin and his Loyalists, most of whom were former Scots Highlanders who had settled in North Carolina's back country, were met on February 27 about eighteen miles north of Wilmington by a force of about 1,000 rebel militiamen. There, at Moore's Creek bridge, the rebels had dug their defensive positions.

At first the rebels, marching out from Wilmington, had crossed the bridge and dug in beyond it. Then, realizing their mistake in preparing to fight with their backs to the swollen creek, they withdrew and dug new positions with the creek between them and the approaching enemy. When the Loyalists arrived on the scene and saw the empty first positions, they assumed the rebels had fled. Charging across the bridge, the Tories were mowed down, losing half of their men. There were only two rebel casualties, one killed and one wounded.

The Tory disaster at Moore's Creek bridge not only kept North Carolina loyal to the patriot cause, but also stiffened the backs of the other southern colonists, especially those in Virginia and South Carolina.

General Clinton and his seaborne detachment arrived off the North Carolina coast in April. General Cornwallis and Admiral Parker, with the troops from Great Britain, did not arrive until May. Clinton, having learned of the Moore's Creek disaster, suggested to Cornwallis and Parker that they move down the coast and attack Charleston, the largest southern seaport in the colonies. They agreed, unaware that in doing so they were playing right into rebel hands.

For several months, George Washington had suspected that the British might strike at Charleston. Consequently, he had encouraged Virginia and North Carolina to send a dozen battalions of militia to strengthen the defenses in South Carolina. He had placed in command one of his best generals, Charles Lee. On its own initiative, the South Carolina militia had placed Colonel William Moultrie in charge of building a fort on Sullivan's Island at the entrance to Charleston harbor.

The exterior of Fort Moultrie was unimpressive. In fact, General Lee predicted that it would collapse under the first bombardment. But Colonel Moultrie and his men had faith in it. Essentially it was an earthwork, but an earthwork with walls sixteen feet thick protected by palmetto logs. Some thirty cannon ringed its perimeter inside stoutly roofed bastions. These guns would be manned by fewer than 400 men, but they were hand-picked men. All of them were also well equipped to lay down devastating small-arms fire with muskets and rifles. Powder and ammunition were plentiful.

Nearby Fort Johnson, on another island in the harbor, was also well fortified, as were the land approaches to the city. Here 6,000 men manned batteries of cannon or were prepared to act as infantry. All in all, the rebels were ready to greet the British with a fusillade of shot and shell from one of the most heavily defended fortress cities the British had ever faced.

The British did not come ill-equipped, but their attack proved to be something of a fiasco, if a rather prolonged one. Admiral Parker sailed his fleet of ten warships and thirty troop transports into the harbor approaches on June 1, 1776. After more than a week of prolonged discussion as to how to go about the attack, it was decided that General Clinton's and General Cornwallis's troops were to be put ashore at a point of land called Long Island. This was on June 9. From this point, the British ground troops were to wade across a water-covered neck of land to the rear of Fort Moultrie. At low tide, the water at this ford was supposed to be no more than a foot or so deep. When the men stepped into the water, however, many of them disappeared into holes seven feet deep. The British ground forces found themselves isolated on Long Island point, unable to contribute to the fight.

With General Clinton shouting commands, counter-commands, and insults at him from the shore, Admiral Parker decided to reduce the fort by naval gunfire alone. But the weather grew stormy, and the troops had to be removed from the shore and the naval bombardment postponed until June 28. That morning Parker ordered three of his best small warships in close to Fort Moultrie, where they were to open fire at point-blank range. Unfortunately, all three frigates were stranded on a sandbar and had to be abandoned and set afire.

Parker next ordered his biggest warships into action. They had a total complement of about 200 large guns, which soon were giving Fort Moultrie a fearful pounding. Much to General Lee's surprise, the fort easily withstood the cannonade, its spongelike walls simply soaking up the British cannon balls. Inside, the unscathed rebel gunners returned the enemy fire with a vengeance. Masts on ships went down, decks were raked with small-arms fire, hulls were shattered. Lee marveled not only at the strength of the fort but also at the courage and endurance of Moultrie's gunners, who throughout the cannonading remained as calm as the Breed's Hill patriots had.

73

To add to the anguish of the bombardment, the day was sweltering hot. Aboard the British warships, gunners suffered greatly under the red-hot sun that burned down through the smoke of battle, while inside the fort the heat from both the sun beating down on the roofed bastions and from the firing guns was all but unbearable. Nevertheless, the fight went on.

For ten dreadful hours the cannonade continued. During the course of the action, the Americans suffered only minor casualties. Aboard the wreckage of the British warships, however, casualties mounted until there were some 225 dead and wounded. Admiral Parker himself was wounded by a shell splinter, not seriously, but humiliatingly, for his pants were shot off.

When darkness finally fell, Admiral Parker ordered his badly battered fleet to steal off toward sea. None of the ground commanders had taken part in the fight, but Colonel Mountrie's intrepid gunners had all but destroyed some of the best warships in the proud Royal Navy. The British were to ignore the south for a full two years after that.

At the end of a year of fighting against the British, the morale of the colonists was high. Washington and other colonial leaders warned them against false optimism, but there was no denying the fact that the rebels had severely twisted the British lion's tail and—somewhat to their own surprise—the beast had not devoured them.

Until the summer of 1776, there were still strong conciliatory feelings on both sides of the Atlantic. Pardons had been offered to all patriots who were willing to lay down their arms. There were few acceptances. Earlier, a so-called Olive Branch petition had been sent to King

King George III (National Portrait Gallery, London)

George by the Second Continental Congress. But thoughts of reconciliation had vanished when word reached the colonies that the king had not only rejected the Olive Branch petition but that he had also authorized the hiring of paid German troops to fight against them, and had ordered a total blockade of all of their ports. The first move was an insult; the second was an act of war.

Meanwhile, a young English emigrant named Thomas Paine was putting into words that all of the colonists could understand the ideas that the patriot leaders had been expressing in the Continental Congress. Paine had been brought to America by Benjamin Franklin, another American revolutionary leader, who thought that Paine could help the rebel cause. Franklin was right.

Paine's forty-seven-page pamphlet, *Common Sense*, called for an immediate declaration of independence as the only sane course of action. This pamphlet, and other Paine writings, clarified the Americans' thinking better than anything else that had been said or written to that date. Soon the voice of the man in the colonial street began to be heard in the halls of the Continental Congress in Philadelphia. The message this voice declared was loud and clear: "Independence!"

On June 7, 1776, Richard Henry Lee of Virginia presented a resolution to the Continental Congress. It read: "These United Colonies are, and of right ought to be, free and independent States."

Although most of the delegates present agreed with Lee, many were reluctant to take the final, irrevocable step. But a committee was named to draw up a complete statement of the American position. The committee included Benjamin Franklin, Robert Livingston, Roger Sherman, Thomas Jefferson, and John Adams. John Adams was the committee's choice to write the vital document, but he refused.

"What can be your reasons?" Jefferson asked.

"I'm too unpopular," Adams said, undoubtedly referring to his defense of the accused redcoats in the Boston Massacre. "There are those not only in the Congress but also throughout the Colonies who hate me. Everybody knows and loves you, Jefferson. Besides, a Virginia man should be at the head of this business. What's more, you're a far better writer than I am."

"Well," Jefferson said, "if you are decided, I will do as well as I can."

Jefferson's work was finished by the end of June. On July 2 the delegates to the Congress agreed that independence should be declared. There were still many changes needed in Jefferson's document, however. It would have to be revised, edited, and cut.

Nevertheless, John Adams thought that July 2 would always be celebrated as America's Independence Day. In a letter to his wife, Abigail, he wrote: "The second day of July, 1776, will be the most memorable day in the history of America. I am apt to believe that it will be celebrated by succeeding generations as the great anniversary festival. It ought to be commemorated as the day of deliverance, by solemn acts of devotion to God Almighty. It ought to be solemnized with pomp and parade, with shows, games, sports, guns, bells, bonfires, and illuminations, from one end of the continent to the other, from this time forward, for evermore."

It is, of course, July 4, the date on which the Declaration of Independence—with all of its changes and modifications—was approved and signed by all fifty-six delegates of all thirteen colonies that is today celebrated as Adams suggested.

John Hancock signed his name with a bold flourish. His is the clearest signature on the document. As he did so, Hancock said, "There, I guess King George will be able to read that."

And so, on a bright, clear day in July, 1776, the die was finally cast, the deed at last was done. Soon afterward copies of the Declaration of Independence were printed and distributed throughout the new thirteen states. It was read not only to public assemblies but also to troops of the Continental army. The response was immediate and enthusiastic. King George was burned in effigy in many towns and cities, and in New York City a huge statue of him was torn down, later to be melted down into bullets for the Continental army.

But, as General George Washington knew full well, the greatest trials lay ahead. Thomas Paine expressed it best when he wrote:

"These are the times that try men's souls. The summer soldier and the sunshine patriot will, in this crisis, shrink from the service of his country; but he that stands it now deserves the love and thanks of man and woman. Tyranny, like hell, it not easily conquered; yet we have this consolation with us, that the harder the conflict, the more glorious the triumph."

The first of these great trials, for which George Washington now began to prepare his army, lay in New York City, which the British were about to attempt to occupy.

Six

"But One Life to Lose"

The British had been forced out of Boston and had failed to capture Charleston—two major colonial cities with excellent seaports. Consequently, they had no base from which to mount an attack against the Americans. The capture of New York City with its large harbor would provide such a base. It could also be the first step in separating New England from the rest of the colonies, along the line that ran from New York City up the Hudson River to Lake Champlain and so into Canada.

The two Howe brothers were given major roles in this British campaign. General William Howe brought his forces down from Halifax, Nova Scotia. He was joined by his brother, Admiral "Black Dick" Howe, and thousands of Hessians from Europe, along with the ships and men

General William Howe (Brown Brothers)

that had taken part in the abortive attempt on Charleston. All in all, General Howe had more than 30,000 well-armed, well-equipped troops for an amphibious attack. General Washington had fewer than 20,000 defensive troops, most of them poorly equipped, untrained militiamen.

Late in August, 1776, Admiral Howe's great armada of thirty warships manned by 10,000 sailors—the largest show of seapower the Americans had ever seen—escorted 400 troop transports carrying the invading British and Hessian troops toward shore. On August 22 the first assault wave of 20,000 troops began to land on Staten Island.

Critics have pointed out that Washington probably should have made no attempt to defend Manhattan, since British warships could sail up both sides of the island and give naval support from their heavy guns to the advancing British troops. If he had made his stand farther inland, the enemy's warships would have been useless.

But Washington had little knowledge of the effectiveness of British seapower in a situation like this. What he decided to do was to split up his troops into five separate divisions—another mistake since this enabled Howe to attack wherever he pleased and to defeat the American militia in piecemeal fashion. The separate divisions scattered about Manhattan and Long Island were commanded by Generals Old Put Putnam, John Sullivan, William Alexander, William Heath, and Nathanael Greene. Authority among the five commanders was never clearly established, and, to make matters worse, Greene fell ill with malaria just before the British launched their attack. Washington hastily transferred Greene's troops to the other commanders, but this only succeeded in further confusing the issue.

The British landing on Staten Island was unopposed, but severe weather prevented Howe from advancing to Long Island until August 26. That night the British, under Generals Clinton and Cornwallis, surprised Sullivan's Long Island defenders. Attacking in the dark and depending on their bayonets rather than small-arms fire, the British completely overwhelmed the raw militia. Panic-stricken, the Americans did not stop running until they reached the safety of the 100-foot-high entrenchments that had been built earlier on Brooklyn Heights by Nathanael Greene. Putnam's reserve troops were also stationed there.

Fortunately, other American troops alongside Sullivan's forces stood fast long enough to prevent a total rout. Most of these men, under General Alexander, were from Delaware and Maryland and had fought together in the battles around Boston. But finally they, too, were overrun. Both Generals Sullivan and Alexander were captured. The Americans suffered 1,400 casualties; the British, less than 400.

For a time, Washington considered bringing over reserves from Manhattan and making a stand at Brooklyn with the remnants of Sullivan's and Alexander's troops. He was encouraged in this idea by the fact that Howe made no move toward attacking Brooklyn Heights. Washington speculated that Howe's hesitancy might well be caused by a grim memory of the earthwork entrenchments on Breed's Hill that were all too similar to those on the Brooklyn Heights.

In the end, Washington decided against what he knew could well be a rash, if not totally disastrous, move. With the major portion of the American army stationed behind the Brooklyn breastworks, Howe could end the war in one blow if he succeeded in overrunning the American positions.

Secretly, on the night of August 29, Washington withdrew his army from Long Island. This feat was made possible only by a regiment of Marblehead, Massachusetts, soldiers and a brave band of Salem sailors who managed to ferry some 9,500 American troops from Brooklyn across the East River to Manhattan. They were aided by fog and stormy weather, but it was raw courage more than anything else that made the evacuation possible.

When the British looked up at the American positions the next morning, they saw no activity there. When they cautiously attacked, they found that the entrenchments were empty. While General Howe's victory was not completely hollow—he was later knighted for this effort—neither was it completely successful, for Washington had saved his army to fight again another day.

Nevertheless, General Howe felt that this engagement had been so decisive that he decided to make peace overtures to the rebels through his brother, Admiral Howe. He sent the captured General Sullivan to Philadelphia to urge the Continental Congress to appoint emissaries to discuss peace terms with the British. The Congress agreed to let Benjamin Franklin; John Adams; and a young congressman, Edward Rutledge, meet with the British on September 11, aboard Admiral Howe's flagship. The meeting was less than successful.

Admiral Howe began the conference by pointing out that he could not talk with his guests as official members of an American Congress because the British did not recognize such a Congress. "I can only confer with you as private gentlemen of influence," he said. "Do you wish to negotiate in that character?"

Adams replied quickly. "Your Lordship may consider me in what light you please," he said. "Except as a British subject."

Howe was visibly taken aback by Adams's blunt statement. He tried to smooth over matters by mentioning his brother, who had died in the Colonial Wars, and the honor the Americans had paid him. "Such is my gratitude and affection for this country," he added, "that I feel for America as for a brother. If it should fall, I would lament it like the loss of a brother."

Franklin was unmoved. "My Lord," he said simply, "we will do our best to spare you that sorrow."

In the end the negotiations broke down completely. Actually, they ended before they began, since the negotiators had no common ground on which to meet.

And so both sides went back to war.

Nathanael Greene, having recovered from his bout of malaria, urged Washington to evacuate New York completely and burn the city to the ground. Washington refused to do so, mainly because Congress had ordered him not to. Assigning General Putnam's forces to defense positions in the city, Washington stationed the major portion of his remaining troops along the Harlem River on Harlem Heights. Washington's forces had steadily decreased, many of his militiamen having deserted after the earlier rout. Those who remained, however, displayed great spirit and determination in the face of the onslaught that they knew was coming.

The blow fell on September 15, when General Howe sent General Clinton and 15,000 troops in assault boats from Long Island to Manhattan. They landed at Kip's Bay. Here the rebels had built stout breastworks behind which they quietly awaited the oncoming redcoats and Hessians. But once again they had forgotten the British warships. As the assault boats approached the rocky beach, a hundred guns opened fire from several British frigates in the East River just off Manhattan. When the smoke cleared and the assault force landed, the breast-works had been blown to bits, and there were few rebels in sight.

Washington personally tried to halt this second panic-stricken retreat, riding his horse into the thick of the fighting and entreating his troops to stand and fight. His efforts were to no avail, and Washington himself narrowly escaped being killed or captured. He had to concentrate next on getting General Putnam's troops out of New York City, since he knew that was Howe's primary target.

That night Howe ordered additional support forces ashore, and they camped just outside the city. By now Washington had succeeded in rallying many of his militiamen—most of them Putnam's men—and the following dawn they staged a surprise attack on the British. Aided by other rebels firing at long range from Harlem Heights, Washington's guerrilla force inflicted severe losses on the British before having to fall back to protected positions at the foot of the Heights. The British counterattacked, advancing slowly against fierce resistance. By afternoon, however, Howe had thrown 5,000 additional men and a number of cannon into the fight. Shortly afterward the Americans retreated to their breastworks on the hills above Harlem. It had been a gallant but futile foray.

For the next week both sides were relatively inactive. Then, mysteriously, the suggestion that Greene had made became a reality. On September 21 New York City was set on fire—probably by the rebels—

Admiral Richard "Black Dick" Howe (National Portrait Gallery, London)

and burned for twenty-four hours out of control. By the time the British had put out the blaze, fully a third of the city was destroyed.

On the same night that fire broke out in New York City, a twenty-four-year-old Continental army officer wearing civilian clothes crossed over from Norwalk, Connecticut, to Long Island. He was allowed to pass through the British lines without challenge, as the first redcoats who saw him assumed that he was just another friendly American Tory. Thousands of Tories had welcomed the British invasion.

This young man was actually an American spy. His name was Nathan Hale, and he had been personally sent on this mission behind the enemy lines by George Washington, who desperately needed information about the disposition of British troops.

Nathan Hale had been born at Coventry, Connecticut,

where his father was a prosperous farmer. There were eleven other children in the Hale family, but young Nathan was the brightest and most promising of them all. At fourteen he had entered Yale University, where he had beeen active in athletics as well as in the Literary Club.

After graduating from Yale, he taught school until the Revolution began. He had immediately volunteered and was commissioned a lieutenant. After fighting in the siege of Boston, young Hale was promoted to captain. When Washington had called for volunteers for the hazardous Long Island mission, Captain Hale was the first to step forward.

He had not traveled far into enemy territory before he was challenged. When he tried to ignore the challenge, he was immediately seized and searched, and the maps he was carrying, along with the notes he had already taken, were discovered.

The next morning Captain Hale was turned over to General Howe, who ordered him to be hanged immediately.

Hale took the judgment calmly, but asked to talk to a clergyman. Howe bluntly refused the request. Hale asked for a Bible, but this too was denied him. A gallows was quickly erected, and at eleven o'clock on the morning of September 22, 1776, Captain Nathan Hale was hanged—but not before he could say to his British captors:

"I only regret that I have but one life to lose for my country."

These words were similar to those spoken by a character in *Cato*, a tragic drama by playwright Joseph Addison that Hale had undoubtedly read as a student at Yale.

While Howe's and Washington's forces remained relatively inactive in New York, Benedict Arnold had recovered from the severe leg wound he had received at Quebec, and he was suddenly about to go back into action on Lake Champlain.

Seven

Washington Crosses
the Delaware

In accordance with the British strategy to separate New England from the other colonies, General Guy Carleton was supposed to move south from Canada on Lake Champlain, recapture Fort Ticonderoga, and link up with General Howe moving north from New York City.

General Carleton's troops had been reinforced by a number of redcoats, Hessians, and Indians under the command of "Gentleman Johnny" Burgoyne. Burgoyne had been nothing more than a spectator at Breed's Hill, and he was still seeking military glory in the New World. Carleton's and Burgoyne's plans were elaborate. With 10,000 men, they moved from Montreal down to Fort St. John's, and there began to build a fleet of more than 200 barges and gunboats. In addition, several larger war-

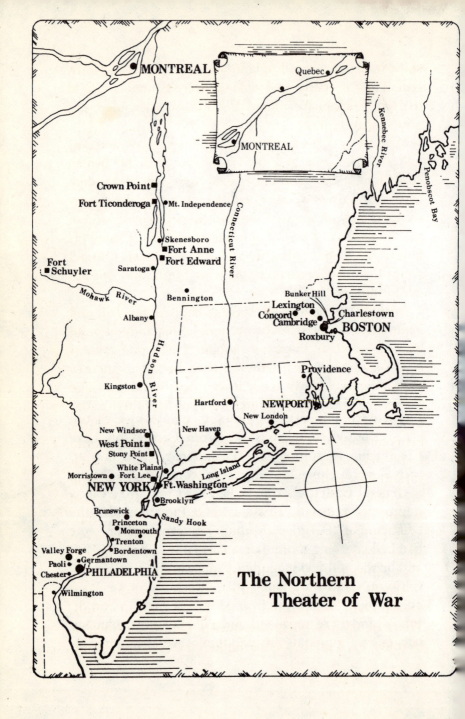

The Northern Theater of War

ships were sent from England and taken apart in Montreal. Their prefabricated sections were hauled overland to Lake Champlain, where they were reassembled and armed with cannon.

Meanwhile, Benedict Arnold and his 3,000 Americans had not been idle at Fort Ticonderoga. If the British could build a fleet and sail against him, Arnold decided, why couldn't he build his own fleet and beat the enemy to the punch? Somewhat like Burgoyne, Arnold was eager to add luster to his reputation, especially after his failure at Quebec. Also, he was still being asked to account for the overspending of army funds, and this angered him.

Arnold's determination was matched by his skill and experience. Before the Revolution, he had helped build his own merchant ships and captained them on commercial cruises to the West Indies. Now he set his men to work chopping down trees in the nearby forests. The green, unseasoned tree trunks were somehow hewn into timber, and sixteen ships were built. Arnold had to bully his commanders, Generals Philip Schuyler and Horatio Gates, into supplying him with sailcloth, oars, other naval supplies, and cannon from New England; but his little fleet was ready by early October. And so far he had beaten the British to the punch! Arnold's green ships manned by equally green "sailors"—actually, they were all soldiers—sailed out onto Lake Champlain several days before Carleton and Burgoyne weighed anchor.

Arnold sailed straight north down the lake, past Crown Point to a position in the lee of Valcour Island. There he lay in wait for the British. On the morning of October 11, Carleton's fleet sailed past Valcour Island, spotted the Americans, and turned about to attack them from the south. Boldly, Arnold ordered his ships into a line of battle. The supremely confident Carleton ordered his ships to attack the Americans at close quarters.

There ensued a sea fight such as the British had never seen. For the next eight hours, the inexperienced American sailors stood off the seasoned Royal Navy veterans, asking no quarter and giving none. Much of the fighting was done within pistol and musket range, but cannon on both sides were devastatingly effective. The engagement took place so close to shore that Carleton's Indians were able to climb trees and shoot arrows and fire muskets at the Americans on the decks below.

Arnold displayed magnificent skill in maneuvering his unorthodox fleet. When sails were shot away, his men took to the oars to keep the boats moving. But gradually the superior firepower of the British began to take its toll. By nightfall, Arnold had lost two of his ships as well as hundreds of men. That night, despite Carleton's attempt to stop them, the remaining American ships managed to escape to the south. Carleton's fleet followed them at dawn, and the next day began to hunt down Arnold's vessels one at a time and sink them. The Americans continued to conduct themselves well, and they fought back fiercely in this continued running engagement.

Late on the second day, Arnold's own ship was sunk. He swam to one of the six American ships that were still afloat, and all six vessels made their way to Crown Point. There they were run aground and set afire. Arnold and his men made their way through the woods back to Fort Ticonderoga.

Once again the British had won what amounted to a hollow victory. Carleton was so unnerved by the Americans' success in the delaying action that he refused to proceed to the attack of Ticonderoga. He lingered at Crown Point until early November, ignoring Burgoyne's pleas to press the attack. Then he ordered his troops to board their vessels and return to Montreal. The linkup with General Howe had failed, and, with winter approaching, no British northern campaign could be launched until the spring of 1777.

Many critics believe that Arnold's actions on Lake Champlain saved the Revolution for America. Arnold did not feel that way, however. He was sharply disappointed at not having beaten the British.

General Gates then ordered Arnold to Rhode Island, which was being attacked by the British under General Henry Clinton.

The day after the Battle of Valcour Island, General Howe, far to the south, finally went back into action. He ordered 4,000 of his troops to board flat-bottomed assault boats and to move up the East and Harlem rivers for a landing in Westchester county, north of New York City. This move was designed to bring the British around and to the rear of Washington's army on Harlem Heights.

Washington had foreseen this move and had withdrawn from Manhattan. He had left small holding forces at Fort Washington, under Colonel Robert Magaw, and at Fort Lee, under General Nathanael Greene. Both forts were north of Harlem Heights: Fort Washington was on the peninsula, and Fort Lee was in New Jersey, directly across the Hudson River from Fort Washington. Washington established his main force in strong, fortified positions still farther north at White Plains in Westchester county.

But, before Washington could consolidate his Westchester positions, Howe attacked, and the Americans began to abandon their entrenchments. Once again Howe hesitated and failed to press home his advantage. By the time the British were ready to resume the action, Washington had moved from White Plains to new defensive positions on the heights above nearby North Castle on the Croton River. Shortly afterward, heavy autumn rains set in.

Howe then moved back down the peninsula toward Fort Washington, which he ordered to surrender on November 16. When it did not, a fierce fight followed in which most of the fort's 3,000 defenders were killed either by Howe's cannon fire or by Hessian bayonets. As soon as Fort Washington fell—with a loss to the Americans of not only its defenders but also of 150 cannon, 10,000 rounds of artillery ammunition, 2,500 muskets, and a half million musket cartridges—Howe ordered General Cornwallis to launch an amphibious attack across the Hudson River to capture Fort Lee. General Greene hastily fled from Fort Lee with his men and moved toward Hackensack, New Jersey, where they were to join Washington. The loss of guns, ammunition, and supplies was also great at Fort Lee.

Washington, meanwhile, had again split up his American army. He sent General Heath north to Peekskill with several thousand men, and placed General Lee in charge of 5,500 men who were to remain at North Castle. Washington and the remaining body of about 5,000 troops crossed the Hudson to join Greene.

After the fall of Fort Lee, Cornwallis followed hard on the heels of the combined command of Washington and Greene. Howe followed at a more leisurely pace, having decided that it was getting so late in the year that his whole army should probably go into winter quarters. Nevertheless, for the next several weeks, the British harried the retreating Americans across the state of New Jersey like hounds after a hare. Many of Washington's men had no shoes, and their uniforms were in tatters. Often the closely following British saw the bloody footprints of the Americans outlined in the newly fallen snow. As the dogged chase went on, into and out of Newark and on toward Trenton, Washington finally began to despair. He sent message after message to General Lee at North Castle—at first ordering Lee and then imploring him to send his 5,500 men, or at least a part of them, to Washington and Greene as reinforcements, so they could stand and fight. But Lee had long had visions of himself becoming commander in chief of the American army, and so he was somewhat indifferent to Washington's fate. Fortunately for the American cause, Lee himself was accidentally captured by a British patrol a short time later.

Washington also implored the Continental Congress to furnish him with more troops, especially as desertions continued and New Jersey failed to supply the number of militiamen it had promised. But the Continental Congress was preoccupied with its own plans to flee from Philadelphia to Baltimore as the British chased Washington toward the Delaware River. Washington's spirits sank even lower when he learned that the British, under General Clinton, had captured Newport, Rhode Island, with its excellent harbor.

In the depths of despair Washington finally confided in a personal letter, "I think the game may be just about up."

Nevertheless, he managed to get his army—now down to 3,000 men—to Trenton. And here, yet once more, Howe's hesitancy proved all but fatal to the British cause. He failed to enter Trenton until Washington had commandeered every available boat. Into this fleet the beleaguered American forces clambered, and, within a few hours, they had crossed the Delaware River into Pennsylvania and were safe, for the moment at least, on the other side. The time was early December, and the winter snows had set in in earnest.

Howe definitely decided at that point to return to New York City and go into winter quarters. He gave Cornwallis permission to go to London on leave and made plans to hold New Jersey through the winter with a chain of command posts. (Cornwallis delayed his leave-taking, and was forever sorry afterward.) Philadelphia, Howe decided, could be captured the following spring. Meanwhile, he stationed Hessians at Trenton, Princeton, and Bordentown. These professionals, he felt sure, could contain any skirmishing activities on the part of the Americans.

By late December Washington's spirits, as well as the number of men at his command, were both on the rise. General Sullivan, who had been released by the British in an exchange of prisoners, arrived at Washington's headquarters with 2,000 of the men who had been serving under the captured General Lee. General Gates also reported ready for duty with several hundred troops from Ticonderoga, and Pennsylvania came through with 2,000 militiamen. With his troop strength rebuilt to about 7,600 men, Washington began to make plans to recross the Delaware and attack the British at Trenton. His senior officers agreed with him.

The attack, they decided, should be a three-pronged one, with Washington leading the main force to a point just above Trenton, while General James Ewing and Colonel John Cadwalader led smaller, diversionary efforts. "Victory or Death" was the password.

On Christmas Night, 1776, Washington led his 2,400 troops down to the ice-filled Delaware. There they boarded the same sixty-foot flat-bottomed Durham boats in which they had crossed from Trenton into Pennsylvania a few weeks earlier. In charge of the amphibious force was Colonel John Glover with the same Marblehead men who had made possible the earlier crossing of the East River, when Washington's army escaped from Brooklyn. Another bold leader on this expedition was Colonel Henry Knox, who had manhandled the essential cannon from Fort Ticonderoga to Boston to lift the siege there. Knox was in charge of eighteen vital cannon that Washington planned to use against Trenton.

The crossing of the Delaware began after dark, at a point called McKonkey's Ferry. It took until 3:00 A.M. the following morning to complete. Every man was sworn to complete silence, and any man who left the assault party

97

Washington crossing the Delaware. One of the black heroes of the American Revolution was Oliver Cromwell (third from left), who crossed the Delaware with Washington on Christmas Night, 1776, to attack the British at Trenton. Cromwell later fought at Princeton, Brandywine, Monmouth, and Yorktown. He survived the war to collect an annual pension of ninety dollars. Other black heroes among the many who fought against British tyranny were Crispus Attucks, killed in the Boston Massacre, and Peter Salem, who was credited with shooting British Major John Pitcairn at Breed's (Bunker) Hill. Salem also survived the war, having served seven years in the Continental army. (Fine Arts Commission in the National Archives)

was to be shot. No man was. Early in the evening there was heavy snow that eventually turned to sleet. The Delaware itself was jammed with huge blocks of floating ice that threatened to capsize the boats and send men, cannon, and ammunition to the bottom. But Glover's Marblehead men somehow managed to get their precious cargo across the ice-choked river without mishap.

Once back in New Jersey there was a nine-mile march to Trenton. This, too, the men undertook in silence, broken only by muffled curses when a man slipped and fell on the icy roadway, or a cannon went out of control and careened wildly among the men.

Most of the Hessians in Trenton were sound asleep, recovering from a rowdy all-night Christmas party. Before reaching Trenton, Washington sent his men forward in two columns to cut off all approaches and exits. As the first Americans neared the center of the town, a handful of Hessian sentries sounded the alert. The Americans found that their weapons were too wet to fire; but Washington had foreseen this possibility and had managed to supply most of his men with the weapon the British had always used so effectively. Now he said bluntly: "Use your bayonets. I mean to take Trenton."

Washington's words were drowned out by the roar of American cannon. Knox had seen to it that the touchholes of his cannon remained dry. Cannon balls came smashing into the town, many of them skimming down the icy streets like lethal bowling balls. One of the gunners manning Knox's cannon was an intrepid young captain named Alexander Hamilton, later to be first treasurer of the United States.

Colonel Johann Rall, commander of the Trenton Hessian garrison, was roused from sleep by an aide. Rall rushed into the street in his nightgown and was promptly killed by a cannon ball.

The American riflemen had finally managed to dry off their pieces and began to lay down a hail of small-arms fire before the Hessians could muster and form to attack. When the Hessian fire came, it was weak and sporadic. Nevertheless, a few Americans were slightly wounded. One of these was a lieutenant named James Monroe, future president of the United States.

Most of the Hessians who did rouse themselves and rushed into the streets quickly surrendered. Others fled toward Bordentown, but these were quickly cornered and killed or captured. In a short time it was all over. Some 900 Hessians surrendered, about 25 were killed, and 100 were wounded. Only 53 of the entire garrison managed to escape. In addition to Lieutenant Monroe, only one other American officer and two enlisted men were wounded. No Americans were killed, but several had died from exposure on the crossing of the Delaware or on the long trek to Trenton.

Because of the weather, neither Ewing or Cadwalader had been able to cross the Delaware when Washington did, but fortunately their forces were not needed.

In New York City General Howe was thunderstruck when he received the news of the American success at Trenton. He immediately canceled Cornwallis's leave and sent him racing toward the Delaware with reinforcements. At Trenton, Washington, supported then by Cadwalader and his men, was confronted by Cornwallis's forces on January 2, 1777. But the wily Washington performed a flanking movement during the night and headed around Cornwallis toward Princeton. The next morning the Americans attacked the British rear guard, two miles from Princeton at Stony Brook. Washington personally led a charge to within a few yards of the enemy lines. More than once Washington's figure seemed to disappear in clouds of battle smoke, as every enemy within range tried to bring him down; but, when the battle smoke cleared, Washington remained miraculously unscathed.

Cornwallis and his men fell back to Princeton, where they tried to take refuge. Washington followed them into the town, taking more prisoners and capturing valuable supplies.

Leaving Princeton, Cornwallis made a forced march to New Brunswick, the main British supply center, where a war chest containing some 70,000 British gold pounds was also under guard. Washington was sorely tempted to follow Cornwallis, since the Americans could well use the supplies, as well as the gold he knew to be held there; but he wisely decided not to press his luck. His men were exhausted, and his food and ammunition were running low.

As Washington and Cadwalader watched the British retreat toward New Brunswick, Washington said, "These have been glorious victories for America, Colonel."

Colonels Cadwalader and Knox were both promoted to the rank of general a short time later.

As news of these "glorious victories" raced through the colonies and reached Baltimore, the hearts of patriot civilians and patriot congressmen filled with a sudden, and all-but-forgotten, pride. Washington and his men were hailed as heroes throughout the young nation.

As Washington led his tattered, yet high-spirited, troops into winter quarters at Morristown, New Jersey, he realized with devout thanksgiving that the long retreat that had begun in New York had, at long last, ended with his army still intact. There was at least a ray of hope in a cause that had recently seemed utterly hopeless. Washington then went about the task of encouraging reenlistments among his men, and prodding the Continental Congress into furnishing him with more troops and supplies for the campaigns that lay ahead in this bright new year.

Eight

No Silver Bullets for
Saratoga

Soon after their failure to capture Fort Ticonderoga in the autumn of 1776, the British had returned to Montreal. But Gentleman Johnny Burgoyne did not linger long in Canada. He was still angry at General Guy Carleton for not taking over Ticonderoga after defeating Benedict Arnold's makeshift fleet on Lake Champlain. He decided to go to London and plead his own cause before the king.

Burgoyne had many high friends at court. As a poor, but popular, young cavalry officer many years before the American Revolution, he had eloped with the daughter of the earl of Derby, one of the wealthiest and most powerful men in England. At first Lord Derby had strongly objected to the marriage, but he later accepted

General John "Gentleman Johnny" Burgoyne (National Portrait Gallery, London)

his son-in-law, and began to exert all of his influence toward advancing young Burgoyne's army career. Burgoyne rose rapidly. He saw several successful years of cavalry service against the Spanish on the Continent and, upon returning home, was elected to Parliament. He was enormously popular in both military and political circles, and his first play, *Maid of the Oaks*, produced in 1774, had made him the toast of London's theatrical circles as well.

Burgoyne had received the nickname Gentleman Johnny because of the humane way he treated his soldiers in a time when soldiers were usually treated like animals. He had even written a paper on the subject, which he distributed among his officers. In it he insisted that they treat their soldiers "like thinking human beings" and not subject them "to frequent and brutal corporal punishment." The British army at this time was so

104

notorious for its brutal floggings, often inflicted for the most minor offenses, that the colonists called them "lobster backs" or "bloody backs." (They were not called lobster backs because of their red coats, as is sometimes thought.)

Many of Gentleman Johnny's London friends had been somewhat surprised when he failed to distinguish himself quickly in fighting against the rebels in America. What he needed, Burgoyne told them, was to be placed in complete charge of a major offensive—preferably the 1777 spring expedition from Canada, which everyone knew was in the offing. Burgoyne had already written up his plan for this offensive, and he gave copies of it to the king and Lord Germain, secretary of state for the American colonies. Both men quickly approved the plan, telling Burgoyne that he, and not General Carleton, would be in command. What they did not tell Burgoyne was that plans for General Howe's proposed spring and summer offensive against Philadelphia and Washington's main Continental army were somewhat different from Burgoyne's understanding of them. Lord Germain was notorious for his strategic bungling throughout the war, and this oversight was a typical example.

Burgoyne's expedition—ships, troops, and supplies in abundance—were ready to leave Plymouth in March, 1777. Before he left, Gentleman Johnny stopped at his favorite London club, Almack's. Here he met a friend from Parliament, Charles James Fox. Fox, of course, knew of Burgoyne's assignment and wished him good luck, adding that he hoped the rebels did not prove too difficult to handle.

Burgoyne's response was an offer to wager Fox fifty

pounds sterling that he would return to England before the following Christmas.

"Don't be too confident," Fox said. "When you do return to England you may very well be a prisoner on parole."

Burgoyne scoffed at the warning.

Despite the fact that he was now working for his former subordinate, General Carleton carried out his part of the preparations so well that Burgoyne was able to move out against the Americans within a few weeks after he arrived in Canada.

Burgoyne's plan, as it unfolded, was relatively simple. Carleton and about 4,000 troops were to remain in Canada. Burgoyne was to be in charge of a two-pronged offensive toward Albany, New York. Burgoyne would personally lead one thrust. He and 7,000 men would first move up Lake Champlain and capture Fort Ticonderoga. From there they would proceed to Albany, where they would be joined by the second thrust, led by Colonel Barry St. Leger and some 2,000 men, about half of whom were Indians. St. Leger's party was to travel from Canada to Albany by way of the Mohawk River Valley. At Albany, both Burgoyne's and St. Leger's expeditions were to be met by General Howe moving up from the south with his 30,000 men. And it was precisely this part of the plan that Lord Germain had failed to make clear to Burgoyne. Howe almost certainly never had any intention of joining up with Burgoyne. First of all, Howe saw little need for such a meeting, since Burgoyne should be able to reach Albany without any assistance from him. Secondly, Howe believed Washington and his main army would have to stand and fight if Philadelphia were threatened, and Howe believed that the only way to end the Revolution was to defeat Washington's army in the field.

Burgoyne's offensive south from Canada on Lake Champlain began in late June. At first, all went smoothly. Burgoyne and his 7,000 combat men boarded a flotilla of troop transports. His warships included nine large vessels with some thirty gunboats in addition. All were heavily armed.

At Fort Ticonderoga there were about 3,000 rebel defenders, 2,500 of them Continentals and 500 militiamen. They were under the direct command of General Arthur St. Clair. It was expected that these men could withstand a siege for weeks, if necessary, especially since the fort's defenses had recently been strengthened by a young Polish colonel of engineers, Thaddeus Kosciuszko. Kosciuszko was one of a number of young freedom-loving Europeans who had recently decided to join the Americans' fight for independence.

Contrary to all expectations—both American and British—Ticonderoga fell without a struggle.

Not far from the fort there was a high, heavily wooded promontory named Mount Defiance, or Sugar Loaf Hill. This the Americans had failed to fortify, since they thought cannon could not be hauled up its steep slopes. When Burgoyne and his officers saw it on July 3, they decided otherwise. Burgoyne's artillery officer, a Swiss lieutenant named William Twiss, who was used to maneuvering in the Alps, said simply, "A goat could climb it easily, and where a goat can go a man can go—dragging a gun with him."

Twiss then set to work instructing his men on how to

haul the cannon to the top, by using ropes looped around trees. All this was accomplished within twenty-four hours, and when the Americans saw Burgoyne's guns staring down at them, they knew the game was up. General St. Clair immediately ordered that the fort be abandoned. They left behind them invaluable supplies and more than 100 cannon. Although Burgoyne ordered a quick pursuit, St. Clair and his men fought a strong rearguard action and managed to escape to Fort Edward on the Hudson River on the route to Albany.

News of the astonishingly sudden fall of the fortress that was America's Gibraltar was received with disbelief on both sides of the Atlantic. When he was convinced that the news was true, King George exulted, "I have beat them all, I have beat all the Americans!" Lord George Germain agreed that the Revolution was as good as over.

Many Americans were inclined to agree with both of the British Georges. Fort Ticonderoga had become such a proud symbol of defiance that its loss, on the first anniversary of American independence, seemed to spell doom to the American cause. Some patriots even suspected a mystery lay at the heart of "Old Ti's" bloodless surrender. Stories began to be told of charmed silver musket balls that Burgoyne's men had used against the fort's defenders. So common did these stories become that soldiers whispered them at night around their campfires, and even level-headed John Adams reported them to his wife Abigail.

In fact, the legend of the silver bullets may well have its origin in a practice that was not uncommon among British spies in the Revolution. They sometimes carried secret messages concealed inside hollowed-out silver bullets. If a spy was captured, he would swallow the bullet, thus hiding, yet preserving, the secret message. It could later be regurgitated if the spy was given an emetic. One such bullet is today on display in Fort Ticonderoga's war museum.

Burgoyne, with his playwright's sense of the dramatic, took particular delight in telling and retelling the tale of the mysterious silver bullets he had used to charm Ticonderoga into surrender. Perhaps he was also recalling his home-by-Christmas, sterling-silver wager with Charles Fox. Burgoyne could not, of course, have known then that, before this campaign was ended, he would have need of silver-bullet magic at a place called Saratoga—where there would be none.

After leaving Fort Ticonderoga in his pursuit of General St. Clair, Burgoyne got only as far as Skenesborough, just a few miles from the fort. There he and his men stayed for three weeks, even though Fort Edward was less than twenty-five miles away. The main reason for Burgoyne's delay was the problem of supplying his army. It took ten tons of food a day just to feed his troops, and this food and other supplies had to be transported 200 miles from Montreal, much of it over land portages. He had originally ordered 500 wagons and 1,000 horses to transport these supplies, but he never did receive nearly the number of wagons he had requested, and those he received were poorly made and broke down quickly.

When Burgoyne finally did move toward Fort Edward, his advance was further delayed by the Americans, who had destroyed forty bridges across ravines along Burgoyne's route, felled trees across the roadway, and destroyed all crops and cattle on nearby farms that might help feed the hungry British. As a result, it took Burgoyne three weeks to travel slightly more than twenty miles.

In desperation, Burgoyne sent two detachments of Hessians into Bennington to forage for supplies. Both detachments were met and destroyed by New Hampshire and Vermont troops who were enraged over the scalping of an American girl, Jane McCrea, by a party of Burgoyne's Indians. Burgoyne had actually wanted to punish the guilty Indians but had been persuaded not to, for fear all of the redcoats' Indian allies would desert. The story quickly spread throughout New York and New England that Burgoyne had approved the scalping. As a result, the local militia were once again eager to be a part of the patriot cause.

Finally, the British reached Fort Edward on July 29. But General St. Clair and his men, as part of General Philip Schuyler's northern army, had moved twenty-five miles down the Hudson River to Stillwater.

Upon reaching Fort Edward, Burgoyne first had word of the fact that General Howe would not come north to meet him at Albany—even if Burgoyne managed to get there. Instead, Howe was headed for Philadelphia.

Burgoyne was not unduly worried, as he had yet to hear from Colonel Barry St. Leger, who was also supposed to meet him at Albany. But St. Leger had gone only as far as Fort Stanwix (today's Fort Schuyler), where he was laying siege to the American-held fort. The next word Burgoyne had was that Benedict Arnold, with a force of 1,000 men, had attacked St. Leger at Fort Stanwix, forcing St. Leger to abandon the siege in late August and retreat to Oswego. At this point Burgoyne realized he was to get no help from either St. Leger or Howe. He must make his way to Albany on his own. Although Burgoyne was not happy with the situation, he was not unduly disturbed. He had wanted to make a name for himself on his own in America, and here was his chance.

Albany lay on the west side of the Hudson, and Burgoyne's forces were on the east side. He decided to make the crossing at Saratoga (now Schuylerville). Although he was still desperately short of food and other supplies, nevertheless, Burgoyne with about 6,000 men, started to make his crossing on September 13.

General Horatio Gates had replaced General Schuyler as commander of the American northern army. As Burgoyne began the crossing of the Hudson, Gates moved his men up from Stillwater to a strong position called Bemis Heights. Benedict Arnold and the Polish engineer Kosciuszko had also been in charge of fortifying these positions. Here both sides finally confronted each other, at a place called Freeman's Farm.

On September 19 Burgoyne attacked the American left flank and gained a small amount of ground. He committed his troops in piecemeal fashion, however, which kept the British from gaining anything but limited success. British losses, mainly caused by the rebels' guerrilla tactics, were large; the rebels suffered relatively lightly. This brief skirmish was called the Battle of Freeman's Farm, or the First Battle of Saratoga.

Burgoyne's forces, numbering about 5,000, were living on nothing but salt pork and flour, except that when their starving horses died they varied their diet with

111

Burgoyne surrenders at Saratoga

horsemeat. As the British prepared for a second attack, they were constantly harassed by American scouting and skirmishing parties. The British took to sleeping in their uniforms with their muskets at their sides.

Out of sheer desperation, on October 7 Burgoyne made his second and final effort to drive the Americans from Bemis Heights. In this, the Second Battle of Saratoga, Burgoyne's forces were quickly and bloodily repulsed in an American counterattack led by Benedict Arnold. Unfortunately, however, Arnold's horse was killed in the action, and Arnold was again severely wounded in what he called his Quebec leg.

(*Secretary of Agriculture in the National Archives*)

Burgoyne retreated hastily to Saratoga, where he was soon surrounded by 20,000 American troops. Many of the Americans were militiamen who had suddenly begun to volunteer in large numbers, not only to avenge the scalping of Jane McCrea but also because word had spread that the British were about to suffer a severe defeat, and these patriots wanted to be in at the kill. After several days of negotiation, Burgoyne surrendered all of his forces on October 17, 1777. In one of the decisive decisions in the history of warfare, Gentleman Johnny had lost his wager, for, the next time he did appear in London, it was as a prisoner on parole.

Nine

Washington at
Valley Forge

General William Howe, in New York City, had decided not to move against General Washington until General Burgoyne had reported that his two-pronged expedition out of Canada to Albany was going smoothly. When Fort Ticonderoga had fallen to Burgoyne, Howe and the main British army were resting leisurely on Staten Island. It wasn't until almost three weeks later, on July 23, 1777, that Howe and 15,000 troops launched the campaign that the top British command was certain would win the war.

Meanwhile, Washington had spent five long months at Morristown, New Jersey, rebuilding and reequipping the Continental army so that it was once again a respectable fighting force. This virtually new army was partly

General George Washington (Brown Brothers)

equipped with weapons, ammunition, and other supplies from France, which had just about decided to join the American cause. One of the most valuable French exports was a red-headed teen-ager who had left his wife and family in Paris to come and fight side by side with the Americans. This was the nineteen-year-old marquis de Lafayette, who had volunteered to serve, without pay, just so long as he could "be near General Washington until he thinks I can be trusted with an army command." From that moment Lafayette and Washington began a lifelong friendship.

Lafayette joined Washington just after the Continental

army left Morristown and moved into Pennsylvania. The young marquis learned that the commander in chief had finally made up his mind where he thought Howe's next blow would fall. There had been at least four options open to Howe—a move up the Hudson, or an attack on Boston, Albany, or Philadelphia. Washington's conclusion that Philadelphia was the target was correct, but he had hardly expected Howe to come by sea!

When Howe left Staten Island, he and his army aboard more than 250 ships sailed straight out into the Atlantic Ocean. Upon receiving this news, Washington had immediately headed for Philadelphia, assuming that Howe intended to sail into the Chesapeake Bay. But then no word of the British armada was heard for several weeks, and Washington began to worry. Had he made a fateful blunder? Finally, late in August, Washington learned that Howe had landed at the head of Chesapeake Bay near Elkton, which was only about sixty or seventy marching miles from Philadelphia.

Washington's reaction to this news was one part good generalship and two parts good showmanship. He marched the main Continental army through Philadelphia, not only to impress the citizenry, but also to impress the members of the Continental Congress. The parade down Front and Chestnut streets was a great success. Washington himself, wearing a handsome blue uniform and riding a great white horse, led the way, flanked by General Henry Knox and the dashing young marquis de Lafayette. Behind them came the proud members of the Continental army, still somewhat of a rabble in arms, but carrying themselves and their muskets proudly, nonetheless. Eyes straight ahead, they marched forward—not all of them in step to be sure, but ready to meet the enemy. They met him at a place called Brandywine Creek, on September 11.

As it turned out, the battle proved to be quite similar to the earlier battle with the British on Long Island, including, unfortunately, a similar outcome. Washington had at his command about 11,000 men, Howe about 14,000. The British had at least 1,000 men unfit for duty, due to exhaustion after their long weeks of shipboard confinement. The hot, humid weather was a problem for both sides.

The Brandywine was a shallow creek with numerous fords, making it possible for the British to cross at any of several places. The most logical crossing seemed to be at Chadd's Ford; and here Washington stationed General Nathanael Greene with a large detachment and ordered them to prepare for a frontal attack. Howe encouraged this deception by sending a body of Hessians under General Wilhelm von Knyphausen toward Chadd's Ford. At the same time, however, Howe sent Cornwallis with 5,000 troops far to the patriots' right, which was defended by several thousand Americans under General John Sullivan. As the Hessians crossed at Chadd's Ford, Cornwallis and his men struck the Americans on their unprepared right flank and right rear and completely surprised Sullivan's men, who soon fell back in complete disorder. Greene's detachment valiantly fought off the Hessians, then left Chadd's Ford and dashed several miles to protect Sullivan's rear guard. Greene's prompt action prevented Sullivan's retreat from becoming a rout. The coming of darkness also helped save the Americans. One of those who fought gallantly in

Greene's rearguard action was Lafayette, who was slightly wounded in the leg.

Washington then fell back on Philadelphia, where unhappy congressmen were once again preparing to leave the city, this time for the little Pennsylvania village of York. They were wise in doing so, for by September 26 the British had occupied the city.

So Howe had won still another victory; yet it too had no major significance. The loss of their capital was, of course, a cruel blow to the Americans, but Washington's army was still intact, and was threatening to attack an advance detachment of Hessians and redcoat regulars at nearby Germantown.

Before the Battle of Germantown, however, the British surprised General Anthony Wayne and 1,500 men at nearby Paoli on September 20. In this night bayonet battle Wayne suffered several hundred casualties.

The Germantown attack was launched by Generals Greene and Sullivan in early October. For a few brief moments, it looked as if the Americans might be turning the tables on the British, who were caught by surprise and retreated wildly from Germantown back toward Philadelphia. Here they were met by General Howe, who led the counterattack in person. A dense fog had set in during the battle, and it seemed to confuse the Americans more than the British. With the help of the confusing fog and under Howe's firm hand, the American attack was beaten back, and the British regained their former positions. This setback, just when Washington thought victory was at hand, was a severe disappointment to the commander in chief. Nevertheless, when he learned that General Howe's pet dog had also become confused in the fog and was now a prisoner of the Americans, he good-naturedly ordered the dog returned to Howe under a white flag of truce.

Again Howe made no attempt to follow up his immediate advantage, though he could easily have overtaken the rapidly retreating Americans.

Both sides suffered severely in the battles of Brandywine and Germantown, the last major actions in 1777. American casualties were higher, totaling more than 2,000 killed and wounded, the British suffering more than 1,000.

After learning of General Burgoyne's surrender at Saratoga, Howe went into comfortable winter quarters in Philadelphia. Knowing that he would be at least partially blamed for Burgoyne's defeat and really having little further stomach for the war, Howe sent a letter of resignation to Lord Germain in London. He might not have sent this letter so readily, had he known of the dire straits in which Washington and his men would find themselves at their winter quarters at Valley Forge, less than twenty-five miles from Philadelphia.

Though the British and American winter quarters were only a few miles apart geographically, they were light-years apart in every other way. Philadelphia was not only the largest city in America, but with the exception of London it was also larger than any city in Great Britain. Its 40,000 inhabitants had at their command all of the civilized comforts of the day, and these were considerable. The British, of course, took advantage of them, and they were treated royally by local Loyalists. The Quakers who lived in Philadelphia, and there were many of them, were staunch Loyalists.

Valley Forge, at first glance, seemed to be an excellent location for the American winter quarters. Strategically, it was ideally located. Close to Philadelphia, it stood between the enemy in that city and York, where the Continental Congress had taken up its own winter quarters. It was also a good defensive position, located as it was on relatively high, dry ground and surrounded by a thick forest. The forest offered protection, as well as logs for fuel and for building shelters. A good-sized stream ran through the small valley—a blacksmith was located there, giving Valley Forge its name—so water would be plentiful.

Washington's most immediate problem was obtaining sufficient food and new clothing for his men, whose uniforms had been worn to tatters from the recent campaigning. These two needs turned the winter into a disaster.

The winter of 1777–78 was not an especially cold one —and yet, when it was over, 2,500 of Washington's 10,000 soldiers had died at Valley Forge. Mismanagement, graft, and corruption all played a part in the breakdown of General Thomas Mifflin's quartermaster corps, which was supposed to supply food to the Continental army. In addition, local farmers were more interested in the hard cash they could get, by selling their cattle and produce to the redcoats and Hessians in Philadelphia, than they were in winning the war. Lack of clothing also caused severe hardship. In the middle of the winter, Washington told Congress that a third of his men could not report for duty "because they are barefoot and otherwise naked." Here, too, Mifflin's quartermaster corps was at fault. Washington finally solved this problem by placing Nathanael Greene in charge of procuring food and clothing when Mifflin resigned. But Greene, versatile and efficient though he was, was a novice at the job, and it was some weeks before he had straightened matters out. When he finally began confiscating supplies from neighboring farms and merchants, great cries of resentment arose and complaints were lodged with Congress. Meanwhile, the cold and hungry men began to be stricken with smallpox and typhus and died by the hundreds.

Nevertheless, Congress was forging ahead in one area, and this was in unifying the country's citizens. In November, a new constitution had been created for the fledgling nation. Called the Articles of Confederation, the document would not be ratified by all of the states until 1781, but its very creation indicated a spirit of unity in the land.

The Continental Congress had been encouraged to take this bold action by the fact that France had continued to give vital support to America. And, finally, in February, 1778, France officially recognized the new American nation, turning what had begun as a minor revolution into a world war. It was Benjamin Franklin, as an envoy to France, who played the key role in bringing France into the conflict, but Gentleman Johnny Burgoyne also had a hand in getting France to make up her mind. When news of the British defeat at Saratoga reached France, the die was finally cast.

The spirits of the men at Valley Forge were also raised at news of the French alliance which was reported to them by Lafayette. Lafayette was among those spending the cruel winter there, as were the Polish engineering

Von Steuben training troops at Valley Forge (U.S. Signal Corps in the National Archives)

officer, Thaddeus Kosciuszko, and one of his countrymen, Count Casimir Pulaski. All three of these brilliant officers from other lands not only survived the winter but rallied their American brothers in arms when complete despair threatened.

But the most important foreign soldier to serve with Washington all during the Valley Forge winter was a German self-titled baron, Friedrich von Steuben, who had served under Frederick the Great in Europe. Benja-

min Franklin was also responsible for securing von Steuben's services for Washington's small staff-of-all-nations. With a certain wry humor, Franklin let it be known that von Steuben had been a Prussian general, although he had actually never ranked higher than captain and had been retired for some years.

Nevertheless, von Steuben gave the American troops at Valley Forge what amounted to their first formal military training. He devised a system of close-order and extended-order drill and a manual of arms that instilled discipline and coordination in even the rawest of recruits. He also wrote a field manual, based on Prussian military manuals, for the use of Washington's officers. American officers had never drilled their own men, leaving this tiresome duty to noncommissioned officers in the ranks. But von Steuben changed all this, and he got Washington's backing every step of the way. In mud up to his ankles, shouting broken English at the top of his lungs, von Steuben would personally drill the men on the coldest days, and he expected every American officer to do the same. Soon they were following his example. This enabled each officer not only to drill his own men but also to become a part of them as a physical and emotional unit. In a very real sense, it was the German "Baron" von Steuben who became the American army's true father. His "School of the Soldier" was to be attended by army recruits well into the twentieth century.

If von Steuben was the American army's father, Martha Washington, the commander in chief's wife, could well be described as its mother. During the worst part of the winter at Valley Forge, she made her way from Mount Vernon to the beleaguered camp and spread as much cheer as she could among the men. Not only did she visit the makeshift huts and hospitals, but she also tended the sick and dying.

And suddenly it was May of 1778. Winter was over, and a new hope seemed abroad in the land. The American army emerged from the crucible of Valley Forge somehow stronger than ever, and Washington made plans to recapture Philadelphia.

But there proved to be no need to recapture the Quaker city, for the British soon evacuated it.

General Howe had been replaced by General Henry Clinton as British commander in chief. With the French participating in the war, Clinton knew that a French war fleet could be expected to arrive off American shores at any time. When this happened, Admiral Howe's fleet would be in grave peril, and Clinton's land forces would also be in danger of being trapped by French soldiers, on one side, and Washington's army on the other. Furthermore, their supply lines with Great Britain might be cut.

Clinton reacted by abandoning Philadelphia in late June and heading across New Jersey, bound for New York City. Just a few days after the British abandoned the city, a French war fleet of seventeen ships carrying 4,000 troops arrived. This fleet was under the command of the admiral, comte d'Estaing. Although this force participated in several small actions on the eastern seaboard, it never proved to be truly effective. As a threat, however, it succeeded in forcing the British to remain on the defensive.

After the British left Philadelphia, Washington broke camp at Valley Forge and ordered his army into action against the retreating Clinton. Washington planned to overtake and attack the British at Monmouth Court House, in New Jersey. The force Washington sent ahead to engage Clinton was under the command of General Charles Lee, who had recently been returned by the British in a prisoner-of-war exchange. Lee was still trying to replace Washington as commander in chief of the American forces, and curiously enough there were certain members of Congress who thought that perhaps Lee should have the job. After all, they reasoned, Washington had yet to win a major battle.

General Clinton and his 10,000 troops, 1,500 wagons, and hundreds of cannon arrived at Monmouth on June 26. The trip from Philadelphia had been a grueling one. Clinton was well aware of the possibility of the British being caught while they were retreating toward New York City in a long, drawn-out column. He constantly had to remind Cornwallis to keep the rear guard on the alert against surprise attack. This, of course, was exactly what Washington had in mind, and he had impressed the importance of his orders on Lee, who was advancing steadily with several thousand men. Several miles to the rear, Washington followed with the main body of American troops, an additional 8,000 to 9,000 men. The American army, despite the bitter winter at Valley Forge, had been built up both in numbers and in spirit, and Washington felt confident of the outcome of the battle. Eagerly, he awaited word that Lee had made contact with Cornwallis and Clinton's rear guard.

When the British reached Monmouth, their rear guard dispersed defensively. They were well prepared for the expected attack. At this point, Lee sent word back to Washington that the British were about to attack him and demanded reinforcements! Washington was furious at what he recognized as Lee's delaying tactics.

Before dawn on the morning of June 28—it was to be a fearfully hot day—Clinton began to move his main body of troops out of Monmouth, on the continued retreat to New York City. Their movement was still screened and protected by the British rear guard. Lee then ordered what he apparently intended to be an attack, but his series of orders, counterorders, commands, and countercommands indicated clearly that he actually had no plan of attack.

A totally confused and confusing series of actions followed, which finally ended with Lee and his several thousand men retreating, until they ran into the oncoming Washington with the main American army. In writing about the encounter some years later, Lafayette said Washington called Lee "a damned poltroon." Other observers agreed that was the least Washington called Lee. General Charles Scott, who was on hand for the meeting, later reported that Washington started off calmly enough by inquiring of Lee, "I desire to know, sir, what is the reason, whence arises this confusion?" Lee began to alibi by blaming and berating his men. At this juncture, General Scott said, Washington exhibited a monumental display of temper, blistering Lee for blaming others for his own mistakes.

"Yes, sir," General Scott said, "the good General Washington swore that day till the leaves shook on the trees. Charming! Delightful! Never have I enjoyed swearing so much before or since. Sir, on that memorable day, he swore like an angel from heaven."

But in the end it was not temper that could save the day. The Battle of Monmouth ended indecisively, with the British moving out quietly toward Sandy Hook, where they could cross to Manhattan and Staten Island. The Americans licked their wounds in the farm fields around Monmouth, ordered by General Washington to forget that day's futile fighting. That night, worn out himself, the general looked about for a suitable place to

lie down. Under a tree he recognized an exhausted Lafayette, sound asleep. Lying down beside the young marquis, Washington used his own cloak for a blanket,
spreading it over the two of them.

Casualties on both sides were not terribly high, and a
number of these were caused by heatstroke. The Americans had suffered 69 killed, 160 wounded, and 37 dead
from heatstroke. British losses were 147 dead, 170
wounded, and 60 dead from the heat. The horses of
several of the commanders, including Washington's, had
also died from the heat.

After the Battle of Monmouth, General Lee demanded
a court-martial. Washington granted him his wish, and
Lee was shortly afterward dismissed from the service.

The Battle of Monmouth—win, lose, or draw—proved
to be the last confrontation between the main British and
American armies during the Revolutionary War. From
this point forward, all key land engagements—and there
were to be several—would be fought by relatively small
units or detachments, and these would be fought mainly
in the south and west.

There were also some all-important battles yet to be
fought at sea, where Great Britain concentrated on waging a naval war, first against France during 1778, and
then, in 1779 and 1780, against France and Spain. The
fledgling American navy was to play an important role in
these actions on the high seas, but the biggest American
role by far would be played by intrepid Yankee sea captains and their crews sailing and fighting in privateers.

Ten

The War at Sea

The American navy was born late in 1775. Its father was John Adams. He was the chairman of the naval committee established by the Continental Congress. As the chairman of this committee, Adams wrote the rules for the naval service and got the Congress to establish a naval policy. In fact, he was so tireless and so successful in founding the American navy that, in recognition of his efforts, there has always been a United States warship named the *John Adams,* from the American Revolution until today.

In October 1775, the Continental Congress ordered thirteen ships of between twenty-four to thirty-two guns to be built. Eventually this order was carried out, but by the end of the war all of the ships had been either captured or burned to avoid capture. Congress also bought eight merchant vessels and had them armed, and France and several of the colonies who had their own navies furnished forty or fifty additional ships. This small navy managed to sink or capture more than 200 British ships during the war. The British, on the other hand, had a war fleet of just under 300 ships at the start of the conflict and almost 600 at the war's end. When the Revolution began, the Royal Navy was actually at low ebb. When France, and later Spain, joined the conflict, turning it into a world war, Great Britain rapidly built up her war fleet to protect her interests not only in America but also elsewhere on the high seas.

It was actually American privateers that were the most successful against the enemy, sinking or capturing between 600 and 700 British vessels during the war. Privateers were privately owned, armed merchant vessels to whose captains Congress or the individual colonies issued special permits—called letters of marque—for raiding enemy commerce. The privateer captains and their crews were awarded prize money for raiding enemy commerce and capturing merchantmen, although in many cases they simply sold the captured ships in European ports and kept the money themselves. It was not surprising, therefore, that most seamen preferred the privateer service to that of the colonial or national navies. Some 2,000 privateers saw service from 1775 to the end of the war. Nevertheless, the large maritime colonies maintained navies of their own, and Connecticut, Massachusetts, and Rhode Island had sizable fleets throughout the war.

Rhode Island's Esek Hopkins was the American navy's

first commander in chief. The first captains were Dudley Saltonstall, Abraham Whipple, Nicholas Biddle, and Esek Hopkins's son, John B. Hopkins. The first man to be appointed a naval lieutenant was John Paul Jones, who was to prove to be a genius at waging war at sea.

In the spring of 1776, ships of the Massachusetts navy and several privateers had their first success against enemy shipping when they captured several British vessels entering Boston harbor. That same spring Esek Hopkins and a small fleet, with John Paul Jones as one of the officers in command, raided the Bahamas and captured a hundred cannon and a large quantity of military stores. After this action, Jones was promoted to captain and placed in command of the *Hazard*. That summer he captured sixteen enemy vessels, and his name was on the way to becoming a household word.

Interestingly, his name had not been "Jones" to begin with, but simply John Paul. Born in Scotland, he had served in the British merchant navy until 1773, when he came to the future United States and settled at Fredericksburg, Virginia. It was at this time that he added the Jones to his name, probably because he wanted to conceal his identity. Before leaving the British merchant service, he had killed a sailor serving under him who had refused to obey orders and threatened all of the other ship's officers. When the American Revolution began Jones immediately volunteered.

Jones had other successes at sea in 1776, and in 1777 was put in command of a new frigate, the *Ranger*. The *Ranger* was the first armed warship to display the American national flag.

On Saturday, June 14, 1777, the Continental Congress

131

The Legendary "First American Flag" (Minor Congressional Committee in the National Archives)

had passed a resolution stating: "That the flag of the thirteen United States be thirteen stripes, alternately red and white; that the Union be thirteen stars, white in a blue field, representing a new constellation."

There is some debate as to whether it was this flag or the one immediately preceding it—the so-called Jack-and-Stripes or Continental Colors—that Jones raised over the *Ranger* when he took command. The Jack-and-Stripes flag—with a jack in the union rather than stars—was a transition flag between the British Union Jack and the American Stars and Stripes. Jones always claimed that he had hoisted the latter, and it was under this proud banner that the *Ranger*'s list of prizes steadily mounted.

Other American naval heroes of this period included Captain Lambert Wickes, who was in command of the ship that fought its way safely across the Atlantic, bringing Benjamin Franklin to France, so that he could persuade her to join America in the war; Captain Gustavus Conyngham, who captured so many prizes off the British coast that British shipping was no longer considered safe in the English channel; Captain William Johnston, whose little ship *Lexington* was the first to fly the American flag in a victory at sea, which was won over an armed merchant vessel; and Captain Joshua Barney, who had been a sailor since his early teens and who became one of the most successful of all captains during the Revolution. His ship, the sixteen-gun *Huyder-Ally,* with a crew of 100 men, captured the British twenty-gun sloop-of-war *General Monk* and 200 men in one of the most celebrated sea fights of the war. Barney was later captured by the British after an unsuccessful engagement, spent a year in an English prison, and then escaped to return home and fight again. Barney was just one of 1,500 American seamen imprisoned at Portsmouth in England. It was principally the successes of John Paul Jones that enabled the Americans to force the British into agreeing to a prisoner exchange, in which many of these men were freed.

As captain of the *Ranger,* Jones not only captured dozens of prizes but also hundreds of British seamen. In addition, he took particular delight in twisting the British lion's tail by actually landing in the British Isles and invading a nobleman's home. This feat took place in April of 1778, when Jones captured the English ship *Drake* off the coast of Scotland. After capturing the *Drake,* Jones and his crew landed on the Scottish coast and invaded the home of the earl of Selkirk, from which the crew of the *Ranger* stole the earl's family silver service. When he had lived in Scotland, Jones had worked for the earl. After the raid, Jones bought back the silver plate from his crew and sent it with a personal note of apology to the countess of Selkirk. A nation of sailors, the British could only admire Jones for his bold action, although there was some talk in Parliament of declaring Jones and his crew pirates.

Shortly after this incident, Jones gave up command of the *Ranger* because he was led to believe that he would be given a much larger warship, and that he and Lafayette were to plan an amphibious invasion of Great Britain. Lafayette was to command the land forces, and Jones was to command the naval forces for the invasion. The top French command, however, disapproved of this daring plan, and Jones found himself without a ship. Finally, in February of 1779—after pleading his own case for months in Paris—Jones was given an old merchant vessel that had been in the India trade. This "East India-man," as she was called, was fitted out by Jones as a two-decked frigate carrying forty-two guns and bearing the name *Bonhomme Richard*, the French translation of Benjamin Franklin's "Poor Richard" in his book, *Poor Richard's Almanack*. Jones greatly admired Franklin, and Franklin in turn was pleased to have the ship of America's most intrepid sea captain named after him.

Jones set sail from France in the *Bonhomme Richard* accompanied by the *Alliance,* an American ship, and several French vessels. This somewhat motley squadron succeeded in capturing several prizes, and then, in September, 1779, they sailed around the north of Scotland

134

and down the east coast. There, in the North Sea just off Flamborough Head, on the early evening of September 23, Jones encountered several British merchantmen being escorted by the fifty-gun frigate *Serapis* and the twenty-gun *Countess of Scarborough*. The British convoy was under the command of Captain Richard Pearson.

The *Richard* and *Serapis* immediately engaged one another, Jones sailing his ship in close to the enemy to avoid the heavier guns of the *Serapis*. Much of the fighting from this point on was with swords, pistols, and grenades. As soon as the two ships were close enough to do so, Jones ordered his men to lash the *Richard* to the *Serapis*—"So the *Serapis* could not escape," Jones later explained.

Soon there was hand-to-hand fighting on the decks, as crews leaped from one ship to the other. While he still had heavy guns capable of being fired, Jones ordered his gunners to rake the decks of the *Serapis* fore and aft, and even helped load and aim the cannon himself. Finally, however, the *Richard*'s guns began to falter, and the guns of the *Serapis* began firing heavy shells which tore away all of the *Richard*'s rigging and all but destroyed the planking on her sides. The *Richard* began to list badly, but, lashed to the *Serapis,* she managed to stay afloat. As the *Richard*'s guns fell silent, Captain Pearson called to Jones: "Has your ship struck its colors?"

Jones's epic reply came booming back above the noise of the battle: "I have not yet begun to fight!"

By now darkness had fallen, but a moon was up and the fierce battle raged for two more hours in the moonlight.

It was brought to an end by several sailors on the

135

Seafight between the Bonhomme Richard *and the* Serapis *(Brown Brothers)*

Richard, who crawled out on one of the few remaining spars and succeeded in throwing grenades down the open hatchways of the *Serapis.* These grenades exploded in the ship's powder stores, killing virtually all of the British below decks. A few moments later, the main mast of the *Serapis* toppled into the water. Pearson had no choice but to surrender, and he hauled down his ship's colors himself. The action was so close, however, that when the cry went up, "She's struck her colors!" several men aboard the *Serapis* thought it was the *Richard* that had surrendered.

Jones boarded the *Serapis* and took it and the *Scarborough*—which had done little more than skirt the edges of the battle and had surrendered earlier in the engagement—into port in Holland. Unfortunately, the *Bonhomme Richard* was so badly battered in the fighting that it sank the following day.

Jones was the hero of the hour, not only at home, but in all of the courts of Europe. Much of the engagement had taken place so close to land that many spectators witnessed at least a part of it, and they helped spread the story of the legendary battle. Jones's defiant words, "I have not yet begun to fight," were repeated over and over again and eventually became a slogan of the United States Navy. The French even went so far as to ask Jones to take over command of the French navy, but he politely refused. He was also offered a considerable sum of money as an award. This he turned over to his crew to divide among themselves, even though he was far from being a well-to-do man, and Congress had neglected to pay his salary for several years.

Although Jones was officially a United States Navy officer, he continued to sail as a daring commerce raider throughout the remainder of the war. Few privateer captains could match Jones's record in capturing prizes, but among them the privateer captains and their crews inflicted so much damage on Great Britain's commerce that British merchants gradually became bitterly opposed to the war. Marine insurance skyrocketed to the point where virtually no shipowner could afford it. Meanwhile, the privateers, while advancing the American cause of liberty, also advanced their own fortunes, growing rich during the final years of the Revolution. Little or none of the money they received ever found its way into the needy war chest of the Continental Congress.

Some historians have stated that as many as 70,000 New Englanders were engaged in privateering, although no accurate records were ever kept. It is interesting to note that at no one time were there 70,000 men in the Continental army and the militia on land. To be sure, at different times there were almost 90,000 Continentals and militia on the army rolls, but 70,000 were never in service at any *one* time, and terms of service were quite short—usually only a matter of a few weeks or a few months at the most.

It is also interesting to note that in the year 1777—a year for which the records are most accurate—the British navy numbered just 87,000 officers and men. Man for man, the sea forces of Great Britain and America were almost equal, and, in the Atlantic Ocean, the Americans quite probably outnumbered the British, for the Royal Navy also served in the East Indies and on other stations.

On May 11, 1790, General Knox gave the report— shown below—to Congress, listing the number of men in the Continental army year by year. The number of militiamen is purely an estimate. The mistake should not be made of obtaining a total figure of the Continental forces by adding up the yearly figures. This fails to take into consideration the fact that a man serving for several years is counted in each year:

Year	Continentals	Militia
1775	29,443	37,623
1776	46,891	42,760
1777	34,820	33,900
1778	32,899	18,153
1779	27,699	17,485
1780	21,015	21,811
1781	33,408	16,048
1782	14,256	3,750
1783	13,476	None

Eleven

"Tarleton's Quarter"

While the war was raging at sea, the American and British main armies conducted no offensives in the north for more than a year—from mid-1778 to beyond mid-1779. General Clinton and the British remained on the defensive in New York City, sending out only occasional skirmishing parties in an effort to draw Washington into a major battle. But Washington ignored these probes for the most part, remaining warily on the alert and contenting himself with sending Colonel Anthony Wayne and Major "Lighthorse Harry" Lee, with small bodies of troops, to destroy any serious threats. Washington's headquarters were at West Point, and his army was encamped in an arc on both sides of the Hudson River.

Meanwhile, America's frontiers to the west and south

were aflame. There had been border warfare in the west against the Indians since before the Revolution. In 1763, the British had issued a proclamation prohibiting white settlement west of the Alleghenies. The purpose of this proclamation was to keep peace with the Indians. Many white settlers did not merely resent such restrictions placed on their movements—they ignored the proclamation. After the Revolution began, the British encouraged the Indians to drive out the American settlers who had illegally occupied their land. The Indians needed very little encouragement, and the warfare was long and savage.

Detroit, which had been in British hands since the end of the French and Indian War, was the center for sending out Indian expeditions against the settlers. These raiding parties had been active on the borders of Pennsylvania and Kentucky, which were a part of the Virginia Territory. In one raid on Kentucky, the famous frontiersman Daniel Boone had been captured and taken as a prisoner to Detroit. Although he escaped later, the fact that a fighter like Boone could be captured at all put fear in the hearts of all Kentuckians.

It was another Kentucky frontiersman, a young, redheaded surveyor named Colonel George Rogers Clark, who brought an end to this situation. In 1777 the twenty-five-year-old Clark visited Thomas Jefferson and Patrick Henry in Williamsburg, Virginia, and told them that he wanted to lead an expedition against British forts that controlled the Mississippi and Ohio river valleys. Because Virginia had long claimed this territory, both Jefferson and Henry approved Clark's plan. Both also wanted to rid this so-called Illinois country of the British commander at Detroit, Henry Hamilton. Hamilton, who was known as the "hair buyer," had been ordered by Lord Germain to encourage the Indians to attack the American settlers by offering the Indians money for the white men's scalps.

In the spring of 1778, Clark and 150 handpicked men, called Long Knives, set off from near today's Louisville for Fort Kaskaskia on the Mississippi River. In July, after traveling down the Ohio River on flatboats to the mouth of the Tennessee River, Clark and his Long Knives marched overland to Kaskaskia and took the British fort and its small garrison without a shot being fired. In quick succession, the forts at Cahokia and Vincennes also fell. Clark reported to the French in the area that France had recently signed an alliance with America, and that he expected allegiance from all Frenchmen. He also informed the Indians that they could either become his allies or he would be happy to take them on in open battle. Both the French and the Indians admired his blunt candor.

Clark's swift success alerted Henry Hamilton at Detroit, and that autumn he set off toward Vincennes with 500 British regulars and Indians. The journey took more than two months, mainly because he insisted upon hauling artillery through the trackless wilderness. Meanwhile, Clark had moved back to Kaskaskia, leaving only a small garrison at Vincennes. This token force quickly surrendered to Hamilton when he and his troops arrived there.

When he received the news that Vincennes had been recaptured, Clark wasted no time in going back into action. Although it was midwinter, he marched his Long

Knives 150 miles through ice, snow, and floods—sometimes in water up to their armpits—until they were close enough to the fort to see its British flag and hear morning reveille being sounded. There Clark captured an enemy patrol and, after informing the prisoners that he had more than a thousand men ready to storm the fort, he released them. Clark also kept his men well spread out in the underbrush and distributed a number of flags among them, making it look as though he had at least twenty companies of men.

Inside the fort, Hamilton was completely surprised by this show of apparent force. He was further impressed by Clark's brutal sense of purpose when Clark's Long Knives captured an Indian party and tomahawked them in the open, in plain view of the fort. Hamilton quickly came out to negotiate with Clark and shortly afterward surrendered. The date was February 25, 1779.

As Hamilton's men marched out of the fort to lay down their arms, Clark's handful of Long Knives began to make their way out of the bushes.

"Sir," Hamilton demanded of Clark, "where is your army?"

"Standing before you," Clark said.

Furious but helpless, Hamilton, with tears in his eyes, surrendered his sword.

During the campaign, Clark and his Long Knives not only took over the Illinois country from the British, but they also solidified America's hold on it by prevailing upon both the French and Indians to become allies of the Americans. His success in this single heroic effort made valid United States claims to the whole region beyond the Alleghenies to the Mississippi River.

Clark wanted to proceed from Vincennes to Detroit and take over that key fortress. The Continental Congress assured him that they would soon send him additional troops to make that expedition possible. Meanwhile, the Congress wanted him to accept America's thanks for a job well done. Virginia also added its thanks and told Clark he would soon receive a special hand-wrought sword. No troops were ever forthcoming—Clark even had to pay for his original expedition out of his own pocket—and the sword, when it did arrive, proved to be simply an old hand-me-down weapon that had seen much service. When it was presented to him, Clark broke it in half and threw it away.

Meanwhile, the war had been going badly elsewhere for the fledgling United States. While limiting his activities against Washington in the north, General Clinton moved powerfully against American forces in the south. Cities that had proved invulnerable at the start of the Revolution were captured by the British. Savannah, Georgia, fell to Clinton on December 29, 1778. Thousands of Loyalist Tories then joined the British occupation forces as they spread throughout the state in the following months. Charleston, South Carolina, fell to Clinton on May 12, 1780, and soon the British and their Loyalist allies were in complete control of both Georgia and South Carolina. The loss at Charleston was especially severe: United States General Benjamin Lincoln surrendered his large command of 5,500 men to the British. Such a great American surrender would not be matched until the fall of the Philippines in World War II.

It was during an action after the fall of Charleston that one of the most unfortunate incidents of the war oc-

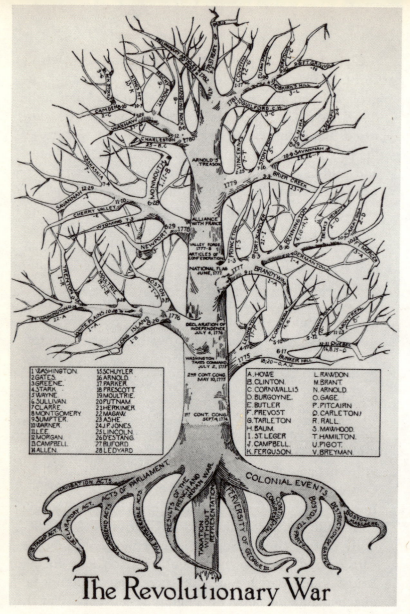

Tree of Revolutionary War leaders and events (Minor Congressional Committee in the National Archives)

curred. Continental army Colonel Abraham Buford's regiment of 500 men was being pursued by General Cornwallis and 2,500 men. On May 27 near Waxhaws, South Carolina, a cavalry detachment from Cornwallis's army, led by Colonel Banastre Tarleton, cornered Buford's regiment. As the British cavalry charge smashed into the American defensive position, Buford ordered a white flag to be raised—the traditional signal asking for quarter or indicating surrender. The young officer who started to raise the flag, an ensign named Cruit was felled by a saber blow from Colonel Tarleton himself. At that moment, Tarleton's horse was shot out from under him, and the British thought their commander had been killed. Vengefully, with sabers and bayonets, the redcoats methodically set about killing every American in sight, despite the continued plea for quarter. One American officer, Captain John Stokes, was wounded twenty-three times and had his right hand cut off. Nevertheless he lived—he was one of the few—to tell the sorry tale of this sad day, the tale of a massacre that lived in infamy in the American army's expression, "Tarleton's quarter," meaning the killing of men who had already surrendered.

After the surrender of Charleston, Congress—against Washington's wishes—placed General Horatio Gates in command of American forces in the southern theater, but Gates was severely defeated by the British under Cornwallis at Camden, South Carolina, on August 16, 1780, when his militia bolted and ran. Despite a heroic fight by Continental soldiers, the day was a major disaster.

By now Spain had declared war on the British—the

exact date was June 21, 1779—and in December, 1780, the Netherlands also joined the American cause. Although she found herself at war on many fronts, both on land and at sea, Great Britain was optimistic about the outcome of the Revolution after her major successes in the south. She was also optimistic because one of America's most successful war commanders had turned traitor and joined the British. This was General Benedict Arnold, who defected to the British on September 23, 1780.

Twelve

Benedict Arnold:
Traitor

The winter of 1779–80 was the worst period of the American Revolution for the Continental army in the north. Not only was the weather far more severe than it had been during the Valley Forge winter, but also Washington had found it even more difficult to get food and clothing for his troops. The main problem was that runaway inflation had made American money almost worthless. As Washington pointed out, "It now takes a wagonload of money to buy a wagonload of supplies." Continental dollars were worth about a penny, and this situation gave rise to the expression, "Not worth a Continental."

Although his headquarters were at West Point on the Hudson River, Washington again went into winter quarters at Morristown, New Jersey. As the blizzards howled around him and his hungry, freezing men, Washington had ample time to review the discouraging past year, and to wonder about the future.

During the summer of 1779, affairs had not started out too badly for the northern Continental army. The borders of western New York had, like the borders of Pennsylvania and Kentucky, long suffered from Indian raids. In this instance it was the Iroquois who sided with the British and were encouraged by American Tories. General John Sullivan had put an end to these frontier raids when he defeated and scattered the Indians and Tories at Newtown, the site of today's Elmira, and then burned the crops and destroyed several Indian villages in western New York's lake region.

General Anthony Wayne had made up for his bitter defeat by the redcoats at Paoli when, on July 6, 1799, he badly defeated a strong British force at Stony Point, just a few miles below West Point. After the defeat at Stony Point, General Clinton was somewhat less inclined to send out any more probing missions to try to lure Washington's army down from the highlands. He decided to concentrate his efforts on the southern theater of war, and to try to defeat Washington in the north by creating a stalemate and destroying American morale. A part of the latter effort involved one of Washington's top aides, General Benedict Arnold.

After his victory at Stony Point, "Mad Anthony" Wayne, as he was called, continued to conduct raids along the Hudson. This activity was abruptly brought to a halt when he had word from Washington that Benedict Arnold had almost succeeded in turning over the West

148

Point fortress to the British. Wayne promptly rushed to the highlands to prevent such a loss, for he was perfectly aware that—like Fort Ticonderoga—West Point, which controlled the lower Hudson, was also a key to the American continent.

Washington's ignorance of Arnold's plans to commit treason was a major surprise, since there have been few generals in the history of America who have paid such close attention to their intelligence services. All through the war, he had sought good spies and created a network of the best of them throughout the colonies. The capture of Nathan Hale had been one of Washington's few failures. Now, however, he had a second failure to face, and this one could have brought total disaster.

The fact that Arnold had been one of the American heroes of the Revolution up to this point was, of course, what blinded Washington—and everyone else—to Arnold's plans. Even after his treason was revealed, few Americans could believe it. But there had been rather obvious signs of Arnold's defection for some months.

After the British had abandoned Philadelphia and it had been reoccupied by the Americans, Arnold had been put in military command of the city. As had happened earlier in the case of General Howe, "The General"—in John Adams's words—"had not so much captured Philadelphia as the city had captured him." Arnold soon began to live extravagantly and was encouraged to do so by local Tories. To pay his mounting debts he began to engage in questionable business practices. It was rumored that Arnold was involved in selling army supplies and public property, and keeping the proceeds himself. He had also fallen in love with an eighteen-year-old girl,

General Benedict Arnold (Brown Brothers)

Margaret "Peggy" Shippen, the daughter of a Tory. Despite the difference in their ages—Arnold was thirty-eight—they were married in the spring of 1779.

Peggy was as extravagant as she was beautiful, and Arnold's debts continued to mount. Soon he began to be openly accused of the misuse of public funds, and the old accusations of the misuse of army funds, both at Quebec and Ticonderoga, were also renewed. The old charges again made Arnold furious, as he believed he had given a true accounting of these funds. Furthermore, he had been passed over for promotion and had been otherwise shabbily treated by the Continental Congress, although he was undoubtedly the best combat commander in the Continental army.

Arnold finally demanded a court-martial in order to clear his name. The court-martial was delayed, and during the delay Arnold, through an intermediary, contacted Major John André, head of the British intelligence service, and offered his support to the British. Major André had known Peggy Shippen when he had been stationed in Philadelphia during the British occupation of the city. André never knew whether she encouraged Arnold to commit treason, but he was fairly certain she knew of his plan and approved of it. André began to correspond with Arnold from New York City.

Finally, in December, 1779, Arnold was court-martialed. He was found guilty on two counts, but was sentenced only to be reprimanded by Washington. Washington delivered the reprimand in the form of a firm but sympathetic letter.

In the spring of 1780, Washington offered Arnold the command of an army in the field, but Arnold said his wounded leg would not permit him to campaign actively. He asked to be placed in command of West Point. Washington granted this request on August 3, 1780, whereupon Arnold again contacted André, offering to arrange for West Point and its garrison to be turned over to the British. The price: twenty thousand pounds sterling and the rank of major general in the British army.

Major André had kept General Clinton informed of Arnold's correspondence, and now Clinton approved of André's dealing with Arnold in person. André arranged to meet Arnold just below West Point on the night of September 21. Before André left for the rendezvous, he was warned by Clinton not to take off his uniform, not to go inside the American lines, and not to accept any secret papers from Arnold.

André was brought up the Hudson in the British ship *Vulture.* There he was met by Arnold's messenger,

Joshua Smith, who rowed André ashore in a small boat. Smith did not know he was ferrying a British officer since André's uniform was concealed by his overcoat. André and Arnold met and conferred in the woods bordering the Hudson until almost dawn. Since it was then too late for André to return to the *Vulture*, Smith invited him to stay at his house, which was nearby, until the next night. During the day, however, the *Vulture* was fired upon by American shore batteries and moved back down the Hudson. There was no way out except to have André escape by land.

Contrary to General Clinton's warnings, André had entered the American lines when he went to Smith's house, he had accepted secret papers from Arnold containing the defenses of West Point, and he was about to remove his flaming red coat and exchange it for less noticeable civilian attire.

Having changed clothes, André stuffed into his boots the papers given to him by Arnold, and on the night of September 22, with Smith as his guide, he started off to pass overland through the American lines.

By dawn on September 23, Smith had guided André to within a few miles of the British outposts. He then left the British major to travel the rest of the way by himself. At about 9:00 A.M., on the road to Tarrytown, he was stopped by three American militiamen. Arnold had given André a pass to show if such an occasion arose, but André may have thought these men were Tory Loyalists and did not show the pass. There is some reason to believe that the militiamen simply intended to rob André. In any event, they seized him, searched him, and discovered the telltale papers. While not wholly comprehending the importance of their catch, the men recognized the various references to West Point in the concealed documents and suspected they had caught a spy. The papers were soon forwarded to Washington.

By a curious coincidence, Washington was on his way to visit Arnold at his headquarters in the Beverley Robinson house across the river from West Point. A few hours before he arrived, however, Arnold received word that André had been captured. Arnold hastily told his wife Peggy what had happened, then dashed outside and mounted his horse, shouting to an aide to tell Washington that he would be at West Point for a short time on urgent business. He then galloped to the Hudson, boarded his personal launch, and headed not for West Point but downstream for the *Vulture*.

Washington, Lafayette, Henry Knox, and Alexander Hamilton arrived at the Robinson house a few minutes later. After a leisurely breakfast, they decided to go over to West Point to greet Arnold. Up until this point, Peggy Arnold had been behaving calmly, but now she had a fit of hysterics. A short time later, a messenger arrived, bearing the papers that had been taken from André's boots. Washington needed only to glance at the papers to realize the worst. He immediately sent word to Mad Anthony Wayne to come to reinforce West Point, and placed the fortress on a full-scale alert. Washington also sent Hamilton to try to intercept Arnold; but it was, of course, too late.

Washington then had André brought to the Robinson house, and plans were made for a board of officers to meet and decide André's fate. The board was headed by Nathanael Greene and included Lafayette and a dozen

The hanging of Major John André (U.S. Office of War Information in the National Archives)

other top-ranking officers. There was little about which to deliberate, however, since André openly admitted to having conducted himself as a spy. During the course of the meeting a message was received from General Clinton requesting leniency for André, but this Washington could not grant. Secretly, Alexander Hamilton contacted Clinton by letter to see if he would exchange Arnold for André, but he received no reply. A short time later the board decided that André "ought to be considered a spy, and that, agreeable to the law and usage of nations, it is our opinion that he ought to suffer death."

Major André's only request was that he should be shot like a soldier rather than hanged, but Washington—perhaps remembering Nathan Hale—refused this request also. André was hanged on October 2, 1780.

Although Arnold had failed to deliver West Point as he had bargained to do, the British, nonetheless, treated him generously. He was commissioned a brigadier general in the British army and given about six thousand pounds sterling. Peggy Arnold was also given a pension, as were three children by Arnold's previous wife when they came to live with him in London after the war.

Arnold did equally well by his new masters. Although his efforts to raise a brigade of American deserters failed —he succeeded in enlisting only twenty-eight volunteers —Arnold did lead a British action in Virginia, in 1781, in which he succeeded in capturing Richmond. But Arnold's dream of taking over command of the British army went astray as a result of the most important event of that same year.

The year 1781 was not to prove a happy one for the British, for it was in the autumn that Cornwallis and the British army were to go down in defeat at Yorktown, Virginia, effectively ending the Revolutionary War.

Thirteen

The Siege of Yorktown

The most important engagement in the Battle of York-town involved no Americans. It was a sea fight outside Chesapeake Bay between British and French warships.

France's entry into the war had begun to prove invaluable with the arrival in America of the French expeditionary forces in the summer of 1780. Their commander in chief was Jean-Baptiste, comte de Rochambeau. While General Rochambeau was technically required to take orders from General Washington, the French general was a skilled enough diplomat to believe he could guide Washington into a new combat plan that would defeat the British. The French were eager to have the war in America ended as quickly as possible, because their major conflict with the British had now shifted to the West Indies.

Washington's immediate plan was to attack the British in New York City and drive them into the sea. He had been obsessed with this idea ever since his defeats there, earlier in the war. Rochambeau's plan was to attack the British in the south. An affable, portly man in his mid-fifties, Rochambeau's nickname was Papa. But beneath his easygoing manner was an iron will that had been forged in a lifetime of fighting in European wars. Quietly but firmly he set about encouraging Washington to see things Rochambeau's way.

Actually, Rochambeau's most persuasive argument was money. The French expeditionary forces had arrived in America with a war chest filled with gold. Most of this was still intact at Newport, Rhode Island. The Continental army's war chest was filled with paper money that wasn't worth a Continental. When Rochambeau generously offered Washington half of the French gold—the equivalent of about $50,000—to conduct an all-out campaign in the south, the American commander in chief had little choice but to accept.

While debating his next move, and futilely trying to obtain American money from the Continental Congress, Washington saw one small but important ray of hope in the darkness. At King's Mountain, South Carolina, on October 7, 1780, a brigade of American frontiersmen, under Colonel Isaac Shelby, attacked a force of 1,000 Tories led by British Major Patrick Ferguson in their mountain redoubt. Shouting, "Tarleton's Quarter! Tarleton's Quarter!" the American mountain men routed the Tories, killing Ferguson and most of his command to avenge the earlier slaughter of Colonel Abraham Buford's men near Waxhaws, South Carolina. Small as this action was, Washington recognized it as the first indication that the tide might be turning in the south.

But at the start of the new year in 1781, Washington had the worst possible kind of news—mutiny in his unpaid, hungry, poorly clothed army. The first of a series of mutinous incidents occurred on New Year's Day, when riflemen of the Pennsylvania infantry in New Jersey killed an officer at Morristown and marched on the Continental Congress at Philadelphia to demand their pay. Mad Anthony Wayne succeeded in quelling the mutiny without further bloodshed. However, a short time later, riflemen of the New Jersey infantry also mutinied at Pompton. This time it was Washington who acted decisively. He ordered other Continental troops to suppress the insubordinates. When this was done, Washington ordered two of the ringleaders shot by their fellow mutineers. There were no further incidents of this kind until the spring, when General Wayne brought all insurrections to a halt after a small body of troops mutinied at York, and Wayne ordered four of the ringleaders shot on the spot.

The mutinies seemed to signal the darkest hours of the Revolution for Washington and his fellow patriots. While Washington was trying to deal with them and still keep his army intact, there was good news out of Cowpens, South Carolina. (The location's name was derived from cattle pens owned by a local farmer.) Here Colonel "Bloody Ban" Tarleton was to have a final comeuppance at the hands of an American force led by General Daniel

Morgan in a battle that is still regarded by critics as a military masterpiece.

General Cornwallis was in complete charge of the British army in the south, General Clinton having returned to New York City after the capture of Charleston in May, 1780. General Nathanael Greene had been in charge of the American forces in the south since December 2, 1780, following General Gates's disastrous defeat at Camden. Greene took over command from Gates at Charlotte, North Carolina, and immediately split his small American army into two sections—one led by General Morgan and the other by Colonel William Washington and Greene. Cornwallis couldn't make up his mind which wing to attack first, but he finally decided to send Colonel Tarleton and 1,100 men against Morgan's equal force at Cowpens, on the Broad River in South Carolina. Here on January 17, 1781, Tarleton attacked.

Morgan had arranged his men in three parallel lines along a low, wooded slope a few miles from the river. Behind the three rows of riflemen, he concealed a force of cavalry among the trees. He told his first line of men—mostly untried militia—that all they had to do was fire two volleys and then move to the rear, where they would be screened and protected by the veteran Continental sharpshooters and the cavalry.

When the British attacked, Morgan's plan worked to perfection. The militia dutifully fired their opening volleys and retired behind the screen of regulars and cavalry. The redcoats, thinking Morgan's entire force was retreating, came charging into the deadly sharpshooters' fire of the regulars. Climaxing the battle, Morgan's cavalry came forward at the gallop, and Tarleton's forces were completely routed.

Tarleton managed to escape and join Cornwallis, leaving behind more than 300 dead and wounded and 600 prisoners—nine-tenths of his attacking force. Morgan suffered 70 casualties, 10 killed and 60 wounded.

In an attempt to avenge the defeat at the Cowpens, Cornwallis launched an attack against Morgan, who now skillfully retreated northward to join up with Nathanael Greene. Here, at Guilford Courthouse, North Carolina, on the southern border of Virginia, the Americans and British fought what amounted to a stalemate on March 15. After an all-day battle, the Americans left the field, but Cornwallis suffered so many casualties—500 out of a force of 2,200—that he withdrew to Wilmington, North Carolina, to lick his wounds.

Greene soon began a cat-and-mouse game with the British, engaging them at such places as Hobkirk's Hill and Eutaw Springs in South Carolina, and then quickly breaking off the actions after inflicting severe punishment. Cornwallis reacted with rare determination. Burning his wagons and all surplus equipment so that his forces could move at top speed, he dashed after the elusive Americans; but he could never quite bring them to heel.

Greene was aided in these hit-and-run efforts by such heroic partisans as Andrew Pickens, Thomas Sumter, and Francis Marion, the "Swamp Fox," who harassed the British beyond endurance in a series of guerrilla raids. Marion had received his nickname somewhat earlier in the war, when he and his guerrillas had made a practice of hiding out in the southern swamps, where the frail

Marion fought off bouts of malaria by drinking a daily ration of vinegar—a prescription he tried to force on his men with somewhat indifferent results. Once, after a particularly bitter engagement with the British, Colonel Tarleton had spent seventeen futile hours trailing Marion and his men through twenty-five miles of swamp. Finally giving up the chase, Tarleton commented, "That damned old swamp fox, even the devil himself couldn't catch him."

Curiously, not only these guerrillas but also Greene's main force seemed to lose minor skirmish after minor skirmish, but in the end they won their main campaign when Cornwallis, "tired of marching about the countryside in quest of adventures," decided to move into Virginia. On April 23, the day before he started his march north, Cornwallis wrote and told General Clinton of his plans. Virginia had long been a vital source of men and supplies for the Americans, and Cornwallis thought he could destroy this source. Clinton was furious. He had ordered Cornwallis to do nothing more than consolidate South Carolina and had even objected to his moving into North Carolina. He ordered Cornwallis to move back to the coast and send half of his troops to New York City. Clinton's plan was to attack Philadelphia and then the Maryland-Delaware peninsula, and for that campaign he needed all available British troops. Cornwallis, however, had been in previous correspondence with Lord Germain in London and implied to Clinton that Germain approved of his Virginia campaign plans. In addition, Cornwallis had received substantial troop reinforcements.

When Cornwallis moved north with his 6,000 troops,

he was certain he could trap an American force of about 3,000 men at Richmond; but these Continentals were under the command of Lafayette, who had no intention of being trapped. Like Greene, he began to play a cat-and-mouse game, retreating before the advancing Cornwallis until he was reinforced with another 1,000 Continentals under General Wayne.

Before the summer had ended, Cornwallis decided he had had enough of sparring with Lafayette. He also feared that he might suddenly become the hunted rather than the hunter. In August, Cornwallis turned eastward toward the sea in order to be near Chesapeake Bay when the British fleet arrived. Cornwallis had been assured by Clinton that the fleet definitely would be there, along with troop reinforcements.

Lafayette followed hard on Cornwallis's heels, but the British succeeded in reaching Yorktown, despite harassing attacks on their rear columns. Lafayette and his forces moved into nearby Williamsburg, keeping Cornwallis bottled up in Yorktown until Washington could arrive to join in the siege.

Yorktown was near the mouth of the York River about sixty miles southeast of Richmond. Founded in 1691, it had become a prosperous little town of about 3,000 people. With its excellent harbor, Yorktown had made an ideal port for shipping tobacco. The Revolution, of course, had killed off the town's prosperity.

Up until mid-August, 1781, Washington was still undecided about a major American campaign in the south. On August 14, however, he received word from Rochambeau that a French warfleet of twenty-nine ships, carrying 3,000 troops, was sailing from the West Indies for Chesapeake Bay. The fleet was under the command of Admiral François de Grasse, whose main responsibility was to defeat the British Royal Navy in the West Indies. Thus he could only remain at Chesapeake Bay until mid-October, when he would have to return to take up his main assignment.

When he received this news, Washington immediately abandoned all plans to recapture New York City. With Rochambeau he would march south; but he had less than two months to move his allied army of 7,500 American and French troops over a distance of almost 500 miles to Yorktown.

Washington's immediate problem was to move his army from off the highlands along the Hudson without alerting Clinton to the fact that the Americans and the French were headed for Virginia. To confuse Clinton, Washington created a ruse similar to the one the Americans would use against the Germans in France, more than a century and a half later, in World War II before the Normandy invasion. In World War II, General George Patton set up a decoy or dummy army in England, just across the English Channel from the Pas de Calais region, to make German observers think the allies were going to invade the French coast at Calais rather than in Normandy.

Washington's decoy army built roads toward Staten Island to make it appear as if the opening attack against New York City would be against Staten Island. His elaborate ruse also included making hundreds of ovens for baking bread so that British observers would think the Americans were preparing for a siege of Manhattan. Clinton did not realize Washington's destination until the first week in September, when the allied army had crossed the Hudson and paraded through the streets of Philadelphia.

From Philadelphia, the Americans and the French continued their march to the site of today's Elkton, Maryland, near where Howe had landed before his attack on Philadelphia. There, Washington's army boarded transports bound for Williamsburg, where the allied armies, including Lafayette's forces, were united late in September.

During much of this period, Washington had had no word of the whereabouts of de Grasse and the French fleet bound for the Chesapeake. In addition, he had had no word of a smaller French squadron of ships that had left Newport at about the time the allied army had begun its march south. This squadron commanded by Admiral Jacques de Barras was important because it was carrying heavy siege guns that would be needed to capture Yorktown. Washington knew that an English war fleet of fourteen ships, under Admiral Samuel Hood, had set sail from the West Indies to intercept de Grasse, and that five other warships, under Admiral Samuel Graves, were trying to intercept Barras off the east coast near Newport.

Washington was so overjoyed when Lafayette told him the good news about the British and French fleets that he threw his hat in the air. (It was one of the rare times anyone had ever seen him lose his composure.) Lafayette reported that British Admiral Hood's warships had arrived at the Chesapeake ahead of French Admiral de Grasse's warships. Hood had then sailed for Newport, where he was joined by Admiral Graves and his five ships, bringing the total British fleet to nineteen ships carrying 1,400 guns. This combined fleet had then returned to the Chesapeake, where they discovered that not only had Admiral de Grasse arrived from the West Indies and moved into the mouth of Chesapeake Bay, but that he had also disembarked his 3,000 French riflemen. Sighting the approaching combined British fleet of nineteen ships, de Grasse moved his twenty-four ships, bearing 1,700 guns, majestically out of the bay and prepared to attack. The British, however, had a favorable wind, and they attacked first, despite their weaker force. In the Battle of the Chesapeake Capes that followed on September 5, 1781, de Grasse succeeded in battering half a dozen British ships of the line so badly that the British commander broke off the battle. Nevertheless, de Grasse kept his fleet at sea for several days, to keep the British away from the Chesapeake so that Barras could slip inside. This Barras did on September 10, safely landing the badly needed siege guns. The British fleet disconsolately sailed back to New York City a few days later. Thus, by the time the allied armies were completely consolidated on September 26, the Battle of Yorktown was all but over. Cut off from help by sea and hemmed in by land, Cornwallis's cause was almost hopeless.

But Cornwallis had certainly not yet given up. Assured by Clinton that 5,000 reinforcements were being sent to him, Cornwallis had barricaded his 7,000 troops behind a series of stout fortifications. However, after the allies had moved out of Williamsburg for Yorktown to attack Cornwallis, they were astonished to see that the British had abandoned all but two of their outer positions. Later Cornwallis explained that he had made the move to concentrate his forces so they could withstand a siege. The allies, 16,000 strong—5,700 Continentals, 3,100 militiamen, and more than 7,000 French—now began that siege.

The heavy bombardment of Yorktown began on October 9 and continued unremittingly, night and day, until the British surrendered on October 17. Before the bombardment began, however, Washington had his men dig a deep siege trench parallel to the outer parapets of Cornwallis's defenses. In one night, 1,500 men completed a trench in the sandy soil deep enough to protect a large assault force. The activity of digging trenches closer and closer to the Yorktown defenses by night, and bombardment by night and day, became routine.

At one point during the bombardment, Virginia's governor, Thomas Nelson, who had escaped from the city before the siege began, was invited by Lafayette to witness the firing of one battery of siege guns.

"To which particular spot," Lafayette asked Governor Nelson, "would your excellency suggest we point our cannon?"

"That house right there," Nelson said, pointing. "It's my house and it's the best one in town. You can be sure Cornwallis is there along with the British headquarters."

This was true. Cornwallis had occupied the house since first moving into Yorktown. Soon he was occupying it no longer, because its walls were filled with cannonball holes.

By October 11, another trench, several hundred yards closer to the Yorktown defenses, was completed. This one also led to the two redoubts Cornwallis had not abandoned when he shortened his perimeter. On the night of October 14, both of these redoubts were taken by assault, one by the French and the other by the Americans led by Colonel Alexander Hamilton. Hamilton and his men fired no weapons, taking the position with their bayonets. No longer were they intimidated by or hesitant about using cold steel, as they had been in the early days of the war. The bayonet had become second nature to them now.

After the capture of the redoubts, the parallel trench was extended to include them so that these two strong points anchored either end of the trench. The allies now held overwhelmingly powerful positions.

And relentlessly the bombardment continued. A hundred cannon were shelling the town.

A few days later, Cornwallis ordered an attack against the forward allied trench, but it was beaten off and the British suffered severe casualties. As an act of final desperation, Cornwallis planned an escape from his beleaguered position. The escape was scheduled for the night of October 16–17. He planned to ferry his men across the York River to Gloucester, where 700 other British had been isolated since the siege began. But British luck had completely run out. On that night, an extremely severe thunderstorm struck just as Cornwallis's escape attempt was about to get under way, and the bedraggled British had to straggle forlornly back into town.

The next day, October 17, the bombardment grew more violent than ever. There were those among both the Americans and the British who recalled that on this date, four years earlier, Burgoyne had surrendered at Saratoga.

In the midst of this fierce bombardment at midmorning a red-coated drummer boy suddenly appeared above the outer British parapet. Amid the thunder of the guns, no one could hear the drummer beating for a parley, but everyone could see him and knew the meaning of his being there. Gradually the guns fell silent.

Then a British officer carrying a white flag appeared. He had a message. Met by an American officer who blindfolded him, the British officer was brought to Washington. The message read simply:

> I propose a cessation of hostilities to set-
> tle terms for the surrender.
>
> —*Cornwallis.*

Only the formal surrender ceremony now remained. This took place at 2 P.M. on October 19, 1781, about a mile and a half south of Yorktown. As the British troops appeared, their regimental fife and drum corps played an ironically appropriate tune, "The World Turned Upside Down."

Cornwallis did not appear for the surrender ceremony. He was either too ill, as he claimed, or too ashamed, or perhaps even too proud—he had never thought much of Washington and his rabble in arms—to do so. In his place he sent an aide, General Charles O'Hara, who tried to hand Cornwallis's sword to Rochambeau. Rochambeau, however, directed him to Washington. Washington also refused to accept the sword, directing O'Hara to Washington's deputy, General Benjamin Lincoln. Lincoln accepted the sword symbolizing the surrender. The niceties of military etiquette having thus been satisfied, the Revolutionary War in America, to all intents and purposes, had ended.

British surrender at Yorktown (Secretary of Agriculture in the National Archives)

That night Washington wrote a letter to the Continental Congress. It read:

> I have the honor to inform Congress that a reduction of the British army under the command of Lord Cornwallis is most happily effected. The unremitting ardor which actuated every officer and soldier in the combined army on this occasion has principally led to this important event.

Washington, however, fully expected the fighting in America to continue for at least another year, since New York City, Charleston, and Savannah were still occupied by the British. What was more, George Rogers Clark still hoped to capture Detroit.

But the world on both sides of the Atlantic had not merely been turned upside down; it was bone-weary of the war. In England, Parliament demanded peace. Sir Guy Carleton was named to replace General Clinton, and his first move was to dismantle British military forces in America. New York City, Charleston, and Savannah were successively evacuated, "Because," as Carleton understated, "of an unsuccessful war."

The peace commissioners appointed by both sides negotiated for months in Paris during much of 1782. An arrangement to which the American commissioners agreed was finally hammered out on November 30. But it wasn't until England finally agreed to terms with France and Spain that a formal peace treaty was signed on September 3, 1783.

The problem of the British in the Detroit area still remained, but that situation would not be resolved until the War of 1812, America's second war for independence.

Bibliography

BERKY, ANDREW S. and SHENTON, JAMES P., editors *The Historians' History of the United States*, Vol. 1, G. P. Putnam's Sons, New York, 1966.

BOATNER, MARK M. III, *Encyclopedia of the American Revolution*, David McKay Co., Inc., New York, 1966.

EGGENBERGER, DAVID, *Flags of the U.S.A.*, Thomas Y. Crowell Co., New York, 1959.

ESPOSITO, COLONEL VINCENT J., *The West Point Atlas of American Wars*, Vol. 1, Frederick Praeger Publishers, New York, 1959.

FLEMING, THOMAS J., *The Battle of Yorktown*, American Heritage Publishing Co., Inc., New York, 1968.

FURNEAUX, RUPERT, author; JONES, THOMAS C., editor, *The Pictorial History of the American Revolution*, J. G. Ferguson Publishing Co., Chicago, Ill., 1973.

HAMILTON, EDWARD P., *Fort Ticonderoga, Key to a Continent*, Little, Brown & Co., Boston, Mass., 1964.

HAYMAN, LEROY, *Leaders of the American Revolution*, Four Winds Press, New York, 1970.

HIGGINBOTHAM, DON, *The War of American Independence,* The Macmillan Co., New York, 1971.

JENSEN, MERRILL, *The Founding Fathers,* Oxford University Press, New York, London, Toronto, 1968.

KETCHUM, ROBERT M., editor, *The American Heritage Book of the Revolution,* American Heritage Publishing Co., Inc., New York, 1971.

LECKIE, ROBERT, *The Wars of America,* Part II, Harper & Row, Publishers, New York, 1968.

LENGYEL, CORNELL, *Four Days in July, the Story Behind the Declaration of Independence,* Doubleday and Co., New York (hardback), Bantam Books, New York (paperback), 1958, 1968.

LOSSING, BENSON J., *The Pictorial Field Book of the Revolution,* Harper & Brothers Publishers, New York, 1852; long out of print, but an invaluable source.

MOORE, FRANK, compiler, *The Diary of the American Revolution,* Washington Square Press, Inc., New York (paperback), 1967; facsimile of many original sources.

PEARSON, MICHAEL, *Those Damned Rebels, the American Revolution as Seen Through British Eyes,* G. P. Putnam's Sons, New York, 1972.

PECKHAM, HOWARD H., *The War for Independence,* The University of Chicago Press, Chicago, Ill. (paperback), 1958, 1963.

VAN DOREN, CARL, *Secret History of the American Revolution,* The Viking Press, Inc., New York (hardback); Popular Library, New York (paperback), 1941, 1969.

WEIGLEY, RUSSELL F., *The American Way of War,* Macmillan Publishing Co., Inc., New York, 1973.

WINSOR, JUSTIN, editor, *The American Revolution, A Narrative, Critical, and Bibliographical History,* New York: Bicentennial Sons of Liberty Publication, Land's End Press, 1972; facsimile of parts of an invaluable and long out of print book.

WOOD, GORDON S., *The Creation of the American Republic,* The University of North Carlina Press, Chapel Hill, N.C., 1969.

ZOBEL, HILLER B., *The Boston Massacre,* W. W. Norton & Co., New York, 1970.

Index

Quebec, Battle of (1759), 42;
Battle of (1775–76), 61,
64–67, 88, 91, 150

Revere, Paul, 34, 47
Rochambeau, Jean-Baptiste,
Comte de, 156–57, 162,
163, 168

St. Clair, General Arthur,
107, 108, 109, 110
St. Leger, Colonel Barry, 106,
110–11
Saratoga, Battle of, 109, 110–
13, 119, 121, 167
Savannah, British occupation
of, 143, 169, 170
Schuyler, General Philip, 61,
62–63, 91, 110, 111
Shippen, Margaret "Peggy,"
149–50, 151, 153, 155
Sons of Liberty, 22, 32, 34
Spain, entry into conflict,
145–46
Stamp Act, 21–22
Stamp Act Congress, 22, 24
Steuben, Friedrich von,
122–24
Sugar Act, 22
Sullivan, General John, 67,
81, 82, 83, 96–97, 117, 118,
148

Tarleton, Colonel Banastre,
145, 158–60, 161
"Tarleton's quarter," 145,
157–58
Taxation, 18–23; see also
names of tax acts
Tea Act, 27
Tories, 119, 143, 148, 149–

50, 152, 157–58; opposi-
tion to rebels, 68–71
Townshend Acts, 23, 27
Trenton, Battle of, 97–102

United States Navy, 129, 137

Valcour Island, Battle of,
89–93
Valley Forge, 118–24, 125,
126, 147

Ward, Colonel Artemus, 44–
45, 47
Washington, George, 42, 71–
72, 74, 78, 105, 114–28,
139, 143, 145, 147–49,
151, 153–55, 156, 157,
158; attack on Trenton,
97–102; battle for Canada,
61, 64, 67; in Colonial
Wars, 41; crossing the
Delaware, 97–99, 100; de-
fense of New York, 79–88;
ending Boston siege, 59–
61; named commander in
chief, 41; retreat from New
York, 93–96; on Tories, 68;
at Valley Forge, 118–24,
125, 126, 147; at Yorktown,
162–69
Washington, Martha, 124
Waxhaws, Battle at, 145, 158
Wayne, General Anthony,
118, 139, 148–49, 153,
158, 162
Wolfe, General James, 42,
65–66

Yorktown, siege of, 155,
162–69

176